# Ciao Italia
## IN UMBRIA

## Also by Mary Ann Esposito

*Ciao Italia*

*Nella Cucina*

*Celebrations Italian Style*

*What You Knead*

*Mangia Pasta!*

*Ciao Italia—Bringing Italy Home*

*St. Martin's Press* ✿ *New York*

# Ciao Italia

## IN UMBRIA

*Recipes*

*and Reflections*

*from the*

*Heart of Italy*

## MARY ANN ESPOSITO

www.stmartins.com

Black-and-white stills throughout text copyright © 2002 by Cynthia L. Jones
Color food photography copyright © 2002 by Bill Truslow
Illustrations by Kathryn Parise
Design by Susan Walsh

ISBN 0-312-30329-7

First Edition: November 2002

10  9  8  7  6  5  4  3  2  1

*Per mio marito, Gaetano, e mio
marito della televisione, Paolo*

# Author's Note

This book is a personal journal of my visits to Umbria as well as a collection of favorite recipes from the region. The recipes are extensions of the essays that precede them, and therefore they do not follow the usual "antipasto to dessert" layout of most cookbooks. All the recipes that appear on the *Ciao Italia* season shot in Umbria are included in this book, as well as others not seen on the television program.

# Contents

# Acknowledgments

As with all my previous companion books to the national television series *Ciao Italia*, I owe grateful thanks to the many people behind the scenes who have given me immense help. I would like to thank the loyal, caring, and very efficient executive producer of *Ciao Italia*, Paul Lally; you make television real, truthful, and fun. To videographer Cindy Jones, sound recordist Jeff Spence, and culinary supervisor Donna Petti Soares, I offer thanks for helping me capture the essence of Umbria, its people, food, and culture, while filming on location.

Thank you to my husband, Guy, for being a constant source of strength and guidance, and for his expert green thumb in planting the *Ciao Italia* garden that each season gives so much delight to our television audience; to my agent, Michael Jones, Esq., who has advised me all these years; and to the dedicated people at St. Martin's Press who shared my enthusiasm about the subject of Umbrian food, especially Senior Editor Marian Lizzi, Publicist Jennifer Reeve, Art Director Steve Snider, Special Markets Director Judy Sisko, and Editorial Assistant Julie Mente.

*Mille grazie* to my many friends in Italy for their advice and help in filming the series, especially the honorable Piero de Masi, Consul General to Boston, Massachusetts; Sharri Whiting; Dottoressa Clarissa Schiller; Alessandro Casciola; Franco and Rita Mari; Walter Potenza; Rudolfo Mencarelli and his daughter Danielle; the Mencarelli Group; Leonardo Brani; Valeria Bosi; David di Liberto; Analita Polticchia; Perugina Chocolate Company; Paola Bravi; Dr. Gian Paolo Armana; Salvatore Denaro; and Maurizio di Dio.

Special thanks to Colavita Pasta for their financial support of

*Ciao Italia*, especially Michele Scasserra, President of Industria Alimentare Colavita, and to longtime supporters of *Ciao Italia* John Profaci, Jr., and the entire Profaci family, and to Jennifer Lionti of Colavita USA. To Joe Pace and Son Grocer, and KitchenEtc.com for their support as national underwriters, and to the Urbani Truffle Company, especially Rosario Safina and John Magazino for their gifts of "black gold" (black truffles) whenever we needed them.

Thank you to photographer Bill Truslow and prop and food stylist Jane Almeeda, to Panera Bread for feeding our television crew, and to the *Ciao Italia* kitchen crew, Donna Petti Soares, Ginny Beckett, Leslie Ware, Ruth Moore, Ellen Pennington, Ryan Joyce, and Peggy Fleming, for always keeping things moving. To *Ciao Italia* director Kevin Carlson, who makes a hard job seem simple, and to assistant producer Jenny Soares, Web master Jim Lewis, and David Campbell of Ceres Street Wines. To the Venda Ravioli Company, especially Alan Costantino and Steve Costantino, for your belief in the preservation of traditional Italian food.

And a heartfelt thanks to the people of Umbria for allowing me to experience Italian life through their eyes.

Open my heart, and you will see graved inside of it, *Italy*.

—*Robert Browning*

# A Personal Introduction to Umbria

The next time you are looking at a map of Italy, move your eyes to just about the center of the boot until you come to Umbria, the region known as the "green heart of Italy" and the heart of the matter in this book: a collection of easy, healthy recipes, armchair travelogue, personal memoir, and companion book to the *Ciao Italia* series seen on public television.

I love this region, which is bordered on the west by its more famous neighbor, Tuscany, on the east by the region of the Marche, and on the south by the region of Lazio. I love it for the simple lifestyle, for the genuineness of the people, for its healthy rustic food, for its quietude, for the lushness and sanctity of the land, and for the spiritual connections one feels with Umbria's most famous citizens, heroes with halos: saints Francis, Clare, and Benedict. Umbria suits me just fine; it has everything that I crave about Italy and want to share with you.

Umbria is called the "green heart of Italy" not just because it is geographically the most centrally located region of the boot but because it is literally covered in green—green pastures, lush carpeted valleys, thickly wooded forests, and expansive mountain areas. Even the name Umbria, meaning shade, helps to define its landscape characteristics. It is an artist's delight: Its undulating hills balance densely clustered and timeworn stone houses. Its wispy grasses move in the wind across meadows like ocean waves, and neat bundles of hay that resemble jelly rolls dot fertile valleys. Mist rising like incense gently glides over the valleys, shrouding tiny churches and majestic cathedrals. And evening light casts a soothing rosy glow that truly calms the soul.

The earliest Umbrians were a farming community that arrived in the eighth century B.C. and were later followed by the Etruscans, of whom we know very little, and then by the Romans. By the thirteenth century most of Umbria was a bunch of small, independent city-states that were under the rule of the Pope. Centuries have come and gone, and yet the pastoral nature of these singular communities is much the same today and is reflected in the customs and in a cuisine often dubbed *cucina povera*, or poor cooking, meaning simple, rustic cooking with minimal ingredients and preparation, and using the local products of grains, olive oil, vegetables, and herbs.

My interest in Umbria goes back to the early 1980s when I made my first trip to Perugia, the beautiful capital of the region. I was there to study Umbrian cooking, and in what free time I had I explored everything and literally could not take my eyes off a city dripping with medieval and Renaissance art and architecture. Every day I would walk from the La Rosetta hotel where I was staying, down the fabulous Corso Vannucci, the main street of the city, and was mesmerized by what was in front of me—old stone buildings with graceful facades and arches, intricately carved wooden doors with great character, historic monuments like the Fontana Maggiore, shady side streets darting from the center and teasing the imagination, and even the very stones that I was walking on. With Perugia as my base, I ventured out to see many wonderful hill towns that make up the region of Umbria, including Assisi, Bevagna, Deruta, Montefalco, Orvieto, Todi, Spello, Norcia, Spoleto, and Trevi. I learned about their traditions and came to realize that each town clings as steadfastly to its distinct cooking traditions as it does to the haphazard hillsides that anchor it in place.

I learned more than cooking from those early trips. The people were unpretentious and proud of their region, and also proud of the way they had kept their simple way of life intact, unlike more progressive places such as Venice, Florence, and Rome, which little by little saw the grinding down of tradition as more and more foreigners invested in Italy and more Western influences began to dilute their uniqueness. I began to realize that in many regions traditions were dying with the older generation. Italy was—and *is*—changing. But because Umbria is an insular mountainous region, it has never been a tourist destination, except for Assisi, the home of Saint Francis. The way of life here has remained unscathed because wanderlust has not been as prevalent as in other parts of Italy, and that is key to preserving culture, customs, and food ways that could otherwise be lost in time.

Many of those time-honored traditions and recipes are the subject of this book. As my viewers know, my focus has always been on authentically prepared Italian food. When the opportunity presented itself for the production staff and me to travel to Umbria to showcase these foods, I knew it would be an intimate look into the markets, home kitchens, vegetable gardens, wineries, and restaurants of the region. And, more important, it would be a look into the very hearts of those who cooked! It became much more than I ever dreamed, because I met the most gentle, passionate people who taught me about the uniqueness and simplicity of Umbrian food along with their deep respect for it. These are the people you will meet in this book and see on *Ciao Italia,* people who were eager to tell their story.

Because Umbria is not as well known as other regions, such as Tuscany, in my estimation it is an undiscovered gem when it comes to healthy cuisine. So what is Umbrian cooking all about? It is about extra-virgin olive oil so coveted that even popes have paid farmers to plant olive trees in order to have a steady supply of the emerald green oil in the papal kitchens. It is about black truffles, those precious nuggets unearthed in secret that are prized not only for the price they command but also for the indescribable taste they impart to everything from scrambled eggs to sauces. It is about wine, too, especially Orvieto Classico, Sagrantino from Montefalco, and Torgiano Rosso Riserva from Lungarotti in Torgiano. It is about protein-packed legumes like fava and chickpeas, the famous creamy lentils of Castelluccio, and grains like the ancient nutty farro, now making a comeback on the culinary scene worldwide. It is about country breads—round, tall, and flat, some made only for special occasions—and for a region with no access to the sea, it is about lots of freshwater fish, especially carp, referred to as the *regina*. And above all, the culinary password for this region and its signature food is *maiale* (pork), superior products that are for the most part spit-roasted or grilled.

Unlike those who live in other regions of Italy, Umbrians are meat eaters, and the curing of such raw pork products as salame, prosciutto, and capiocolla is an art form mastered by the *norcino* (pork butcher), who is revered like a rock star. And the best part of all this is that you can replicate healthy Umbrian cooking in your own kitchen since the ingredients are as near as your local grocery store, Italian specialty store, or the Internet, where you can find Umbrian olive oils, wines, legumes, and, yes, even truffles!

As you flip through the pages of this book, I hope you will be inspired as I was to embrace a genuine, unspoiled country cuisine that will surely win over your heart. *Buon divertimento e buon appetito!*

# Black Truffles for Toscanella, That Noble Dog!

*Frittata ai Tartufi Neri* (Black Truffle Omelette)

*Penne Tartufate* (Penne with Truffles and Cream)

*Spaghetti ai Tartufi Neri* (Spaghetti with Black Truffles)

*Scaloppine di Vitello ai Tartufi Neri e Fragole* (Veal with Black Truffle and Strawberry Sauce)

*T*oscanella, a mutt with a sleek brown coat, seemed charged up today. Maybe she sensed that visitors had come to watch her perform a unique job for which she has been trained from the time she was a five-month-old pup: to hunt for *tartufi neri,* black truffles, a fungus that grows underground near the base of oak

*Toscanella takes a break from hunting for black truffles.*

trees and for which the Italians have a great appetite. Black truffles are synonymous with Umbria and the pride of the region, just as *bistecca* (steak) is the pride of Tuscany, and the ubiquitous pizza is the pride of Naples.

Toscanella takes her orders from owner Mario Martelli, a proud *tartufaro* (truffle hunter); tall and slender with piercing green eyes and a wily smile, he was born in Montefalco. Mario is considered an independent truffle hunter who hunts where permitted in public areas. He pays a tax to the government for this privilege, or he makes an arrangement with private landowners to scour their woodlands. He has been training dogs and searching for truffles his whole life, and he is anxious to instruct me in the art of the hunt. As many times as I have been to Umbria, especially around the area of Spello, I have always wondered how dogs were able to find this unique food.

Mario explained that at one time truffle hunters used pigs to unearth what had become known as "black gold," but they found that to be a money-losing proposition, since the pigs enjoyed the truffles themselves! Dogs do not have such exquisite taste and are first trained to hunt the *bianchetto* (small truffle). The dog's keen sense of smell becomes his guide. From recognizing the smell of the bianchetto the dogs quickly learn to smell and search for the larger winter black truffle, which is hunted from December to mid-March, from north of Tuscany to the center of Umbria. The summer truffle, called *scorzone,* has nubbies, or bumps, all over it, and can be found from May to August. The autumn truffle appears from October to November; it is brown with a brown interior and has smaller nubbies than the summer variety.

Mario said just one magic word to Toscanella—*qua,* which means *here*. This commanded the dog to look in certain areas around the base of oak trees where small plants have withered and died and grass does not grow, a sure sign that there lie, hidden in the earth, black truffles that are sapping nutrients from around the tree. With a stick Mario directed Toscanella to the area where he suspected the truffles would be found. Sure enough, and in almost an instant, Toscanella sniffed, scratched the soil, then burrowed her nose not too far into the ground. She brought up a truffle in her mouth and quickly deposited this "black gold" in Mario's hand. At first glance black truffles are no beauties, nothing to rave about. To my eye they looked like misshapen nuggets with crags and gnarls and bumps all over them. But as is true of the old adage that you can't tell a book by its cover, you cannot appreciate a black truffle until you have your first taste.

Toscanella was rewarded with *un bicottino* (little cookie) and a gentle pat on the head. The glow on Mario's face was almost as priceless as the truffle he put in his leather pouch. It is this team effort, the culmination of all the time this man and dog have spent together in training and in trusting one another, that makes finding truffles so mesmerizing.

Each seasonal variety has its distinguishing characteristics, with the winter truffle being the most prized for its woodsy, mossy, earthy smell. Black as coal and having a smoother surface than summer or fall truffles, their flavor can best be described as that of the forest. In fact, I find it ludicrous to even try to describe the flavor; it is simply unique. Some suggest that it is an acquired taste, but I was drawn to them immediately. Summer truffles are also black and have a white interior; they are not as aromatic as their winter cousins.

As the hunt wore on, I was amazed that in less than ten minutes Toscanella had scampered from tree to tree and uncovered a stash of truffles ranging in size from a golf ball to a tomato. This was the first time I had ever experienced what it took to find them, and I was like a schoolgirl, just giddy with joy to hold and smell them. As a cook I felt the urge to get to the kitchen and enjoy them over a plate of steaming tagliatelle before their magic qualities evaporated into thin air.

Mario's facial expression turned serious as he explained that hunting for black truffles can be a dangerous occupation. Each dog that is trained to hunt is considered a precious dog, and it is not unheard of for the *tartufaro* to have two or more dogs for the task, since envy does exist among truffle hunters and some have been known to go so far as to poison a rival hunter's dogs! Since truffles command such a hefty price, he who finds the most will reap monetary gain. That is why it is always best to keep the whereabouts of truffles to yourself and seek them out at times when no one is looking. As soon as truffles are unearthed, they are sold; many are spoken for before they ever leave their hidden environment by wholesalers, restaurants, and gourmands.

It is best to use truffles as soon as you get them, because they deteriorate quickly. They can be stored for a few days at most if kept in the refrigerator wrapped in brown paper. To clean them simply brush the dirt away.

I asked Mario what was the best way to preserve truffles for a longer period of time. He grinds them up in a meat grinder on a small-hole setting and stores the bits in olive oil, then uses them in such classic Umbrian recipes as truffle with bruschetta, with eggs, with trout, and with pasta. One thing you quickly learn about truffles is that they are never cooked; cooking them would destroy their flavor. They are meant to be warmed in olive oil or used raw, thinly shaved over a dish of pasta or rice.

By now I was lamenting to Mario about not being able to enjoy these truffles at home. He waved his arms as if to dismiss such a question. Truffles belong to Umbria, to Italy, he said. "You eat them here, *non è vero, Toscanella*?"

*Note*: Truffles are available in the United States from several importers. Urbani, with operations in Umbria and Long Island, will ship truffles (see Mail Order Sources, page 197). You can also find jarred truffles, truffle paste, truffle-infused cheese, and truffle oils in Italian specialty stores or online. Although these processed truffle products are tasty, they can never compare with the real thing.

# Frittata ai Tartufi Neri

## Black Truffle Omelette

Serves 4

*One* of the most popular ways that Umbrians enjoy black truffles is with eggs, either in a frittata or mixed into scrambled eggs. This is usually served as a first course.

Beat the eggs with a whisk in a bowl with the salt. Stir in the truffle or truffle paste.

Heat the oil in a 10-inch nonstick pan. When it begins to shimmer, carefully pour in the egg mixture. Cook over medium heat until the top is set. Serve immediately.

**4 large eggs**

**1¼ teaspoons salt**

**1 small black truffle, grated, or 1½ teaspoons truffle paste**

**3 tablespoons extra-virgin olive oil**

*Black Truffles for Toscanella, That Noble Dog!*     7

# *Penne Tartufate*

## Penne with Truffles and Cream

Serves 4

*8 tablespoons (1 stick)
unsalted butter at
room temperature*

*1 cup heavy cream*

*4 ounces grated
Parmigiano-Reggiano
cheese*

*Salt to taste*

*1 pound penne*

*4 ounces black truffle,
grated, or 3½ ounces
or 4 tablespoons of the
jarred equivalent*

*Ground black pepper
to taste*

*As if black truffles alone were not wonderful enough as an ingredient, there is always this rich penne, black truffle, and heavy cream dish to consider. I usually make this for a very important occasion, since fresh truffles can cost more than an entire food budget for a week! I find that one medium-size truffle, about the size of a small lemon, is the perfect amount here. The alternative to fresh are the much less expensive jarred black truffles or even truffle paste. You decide.*

Heat the butter and cream over low heat in a sauté pan large enough to accommodate the penne after it is cooked. Stir in 2 tablespoons of the cheese. Keep the sauce warm.

Cook the penne in 4 quarts of boiling water to which 1 tablespoon of salt has been added. As it cooks, break a piece of penne in the center to see that no white, raw flour remains; this is pasta cooked *al dente*. Drain the pasta in a colander, then transfer it to the sauté pan with the butter and cream. Stir in the truffle, the remaining cheese, and salt and pepper just before taking the pan from the heat.

Transfer the penne to a serving platter and enjoy this fabulous dish at once! I liked it left over as well.

# *Spaghetti ai Tartufi Neri*

## Spaghetti with Black Truffles

Serves 4

*B*lack truffles are known as trifolati *in Umbria. One of the easiest and tastiest uses for them is in this dish. To get the most flavor, soak the shaved truffle slices in a good extra-virgin olive oil for a day before putting the dish together.*

**2 fresh black truffles or 2 canned (if you must)**

**⅔ cup extra-virgin olive oil**

**1 pound spaghetti**

**2 cloves garlic, minced**

**½ teaspoon salt**

**Grated pecorino cheese (optional)**

If the truffles are dirty, brush them with a mushroom brush or a paper towel. Slice them very thin with a truffle slicer, a sharp knife, or on a box cheese grater. Place the truffles in a shallow dish and pour the olive oil over them. Cover with plastic wrap and allow to remain at room temperature for several hours or overnight.

Cook the spaghetti, following the directions on page 8 for cooking pasta. While the spaghetti is cooking, in a large skillet, heat 2 tablespoons of the oil that the truffles are marinating in and cook the garlic until it is soft but not browned. Turn off the heat and add the remaining olive oil and the truffles.

Drain the spaghetti, reserving 2 tablespoons of the cooking water. Add the spaghetti and reserved water to the skillet. Reheat the mixture over very low heat just until it is hot. Stir in the salt. Transfer the mixture to a platter and serve immediately. Pass the cheese on the side if desired.

# Scaloppine di Vitello ai Tartufi Neri e Fragole

## Veal with Black Truffles and Strawberry Sauce

Serves 6

*Salt and pepper to taste*

*Six 8-ounce veal cutlets about ¼ inch thick*

*8 ripe strawberries, stemmed*

*6 tablespoons unsalted butter*

*3 ounces black truffle paste*

*½ cup dry white wine*

*1 tablespoon all-purpose flour*

*½ cup thin shavings of pecorino cheese*

*2 fresh or frozen cooked artichoke hearts, cut into thin slices*

*Thin slices of veal cutlet cooked flash in the pan and then baked with a topping of fresh strawberries, black truffle paste, slivers of cheese, and artichokes slices sounds exotic, and it is! This unusual and delicious preparation is the work of chef-teacher Mario Ragni, who showed me how it was done in his Ristorante M. R. in Perugia. I was a little leery, but my skepticism was laid to rest with one heavenly taste and the twinkle in his eye.*

Preheat the oven to 350° F.

Rub salt and pepper all over the veal cutlets and set aside.

Mash the strawberries in a small bowl with a fork and set aside.

Melt 4 tablespoons of the butter in a small saucepan over medium-high heat. Stir in the strawberries and cook for 1 minute. Stir in the truffle paste and blend well. Set aside.

Melt the remaining butter in a 10- to 12-inch sauté pan over medium-high heat. Brown the cutlets in batches, about 1 minute on each side. Remove and keep warm.

Stir the wine and flour into the drippings in the sauté pan and cook until smooth, about 1 minute. Stir in the strawberry and truffle mixture, and cook until the sauce is slightly thickened. Spoon the sauce over the veal slices. Cover the sauce with the cheese shavings.

Bake the veal for 5 minutes, or just until the cheese is melted. Sprinkle the artichoke slices over the veal and serve at once.

# A Knack for Gnocchi

*Gnocchi di Prugne Secche* (Dried Prune Gnocchi)

*Gnocchi di Zucca Gialla* (Squash Gnocchi)

*Good gnocchi need a light touch.*

$\mathcal{M}$y map of Umbria did not even list Grutti, a small town near the wine center of Montefalco, which was my destination to film a cooking segment with a group of female chefs at a typical Umbrian *ristorante* called Le Noci, named for two nut trees that graced and shaded the outdoor dining area. It was clear to me as we drove through the town that Grutti was not a tourist destination. This town was about quiet streets, vivid purple bougainvillea spilling from balconies, boys kicking around a soccer ball, and a few women standing around and chatting about the news of the day. Yet a friend of mine, Sharri Whiting, who lived near Montefalco, had convinced me that this was the place to come if I wanted real home-cooked Umbrian food—and there was no hesitation on my part to make Grutti a must-stop destination.

The restaurant was homey-looking, with long, dark wooden tables and chairs, and when we entered with our television gear, we were met by Daniella Benvenuti, the head chef. Parisian by birth, she is a vivacious and energetic woman who speaks in rapid-fire sentences, and she welcomed us warmly. She was all set up to show me how she made gnocchi, but first introductions were in order. There were Cesarina, Alfride, Marsilia, and Marina, sturdy, no-nonsense women ranging in age from young to old; they worked together to turn out the daily dinner fare for the legions of locals who came to enjoy country food and good wine. It was unusual to see a bevy of all women chefs in an Italian restaurant; in all the years I had been going to Italy, men had dominated restaurant kitchens in all areas of preparation but one: the making of fresh pasta, which had always been the domain of the *sfoglina*, the woman pasta maker. But here in Grutti it was clear that things were changing in Italy for women chefs. This comforted me.

The kitchen was functional and full of steam; huge pots of boiling water were at the ready for the day's pasta, and a galantine of chicken was getting its finishing touches. Daniella directed my attention to a long table with a huge heap of flour on it. "This is where we will make the *gnocchi di prugne secche*." Dried prune gnocchi definitely did not ring a bell with me as being typical Umbrian fare; they were more in the northern Italian tradition. I did not want to seem rude, but I had to ask why we were making them instead of some typical Umbrian pasta dish like *strangozzi* or *frascarelli*. Daniella's answer could not have been more direct. "Because my customers like them, and until they tell me they do not like them anymore, I will continue to make them." Sound reasoning from a good businesswoman as well as a good chef.

Potatoes were riced and ready to be added to the flour along with eggs whose yolks were as orange as any jack-o-lantern. A pinch of salt, and we were ready to roll up our sleeves. In situations like these, where I am a chef but also a visitor, I do not want to appear too anxious, but Daniella read my mind and offered to let me make the dough. Even in Grutti I was immediately at home. I plunged my hands into the ingredients and made a satisfactory and submissive-looking ball of dough. "Signora, you have done this before," piped up Marina. That brought a smile and a laugh in appreciation of her compliment.

Daniella then showed me how she made prune gnocchi. The dough was rolled and cut with a round cutter into circles, and cut-up dried prunes and even apricots were put into the center of each circle. The circles were folded in half to make a half-moon shape, and the edges were sealed with a fork. These were boiled like regular potato gnocchi, and while they cooked, Daniella and I talked about the challenges that faced all women chefs: first, the need to be taken seriously; second, the stamina it took to cook every day, with long hours on your feet; and third, the need to stay focused on what we wanted to express in our cooking.

The gnocchi were bobbing to the top of the pot, and Daniella fished them out of the water with a slotted spoon and put them on a large platter. Melted butter was poured over them, then a grating of Parmigiano-Reggiano cheese and a sprinkling of ground cinnamon. I sampled them. They were delicious and light; the filling was a great not-too-sweet foil against the mild-tasting dough. So what if they were not typically Umbrian; they had been made with enthusiasm, pride, and attention to detail and authenticity—benchmarks of good home cooking whether in Umbria or anywhere else in Italy. I told Daniella, *"Brava, signora,"* and added that a trip to Grutti should be a must for anyone who wanted to taste the food of a great and caring chef.

# Gnocchi di Prugne Secche

## Dried Prune Gnocchi

Serves 8

*4 large baking potatoes*

*1 large egg*

*¼ teaspoon salt*

*2 cups (approximately) unbleached all-purpose flour*

*1 cup dried prunes, cut in half*

*1 cup dried apricots, cut in half*

*16 tablespoons (2 sticks) unsalted butter*

*⅓ cup grated Parmigiano-Reggiano cheese*

*¼ teaspoon ground cinnamon*

*Here is the recipe for those wonderful-tasting prune gnocchi made for me at Le Noci in Grutti. Why not make them for your family and keep the filling a surprise?*

Either boil the unpeeled potatoes whole in a large pot of water until tender or bake them in the microwave according to your microwave's directions. Let the potatoes cool, then peel them.

Rice the potatoes into a bowl or mash them by hand. Blend in the egg and salt.

Heap the flour onto a work surface and make a hole in the center with your hands. Place the potatoes in the center and begin working the flour into the potatoes until you have a ball of dough that you can knead and that is slightly tacky but not sticking to your hands. If you feel you need more flour, add it a few tablespoons at a time.

Break off a small piece of dough and form it into a little ball the size of a grape. Drop it into boiling water, and if it holds together and does not fall apart, you have the right consistency. Go ahead and make the rest of the gnocchi.

Lightly flour the work surface. Use a rolling pin to roll out the dough until it is about ¼ inch thick. Use a 2-inch round cutter to cut circles; reroll the scrapes to make more circles. Place a prune or apricot half in the center of each circle. Fold the circle in half to form a half-moon shape. Use a fork to seal the edges. This is important because there is nothing worse than gnocchi that come apart as they are boiled.

As you make the gnocchi, place them on a towel-lined baking sheet; do not stack them on top of one another.

Have a large pot of boiling water ready. In a smaller pot, melt the butter and keep it warm.

Cook the gnocchi in batches until they rise to the surface. Remove them with a slotted spoon to a serving platter and keep them warm while you finish cooking the rest.

Pour the melted butter over the gnocchi and sprinkle them with the cheese and cinnamon. Toss gently and serve at once.

# Gnocchi di Zucca Gialla

## Squash Gnocchi

Makes approximately eighteen 1½-inch-wide gnocchi; serves 4 to 6

*1 pound
butternut squash,
cut into 4 quarters*

*1 cup (approximately)
unbleached
all-purpose flour*

*4 egg yolks,
lightly beaten*

*1½ teaspoons
fine sea salt*

*¼ teaspoon
ground cinnamon*

*⅓ cup finely diced
dried apricots*

*½ cup grated
Parmigiano-Reggiano
cheese*

*4 tablespoons
unsalted butter*

*It is almost impossible to anticipate the exact amount of flour that a recipe for potato gnocchi will need. The flour used, the size of the eggs, the type of potato, the way the dough is worked—all these are factors. In making dough you will know by its feel whether it is the right consistency, so if it does not come out perfect the first time, don't be afraid to start over. Eventually your hands will talk to you and let you know when enough is enough (flour, that is). This gnocchi dough, made with butternut squash, makes a thick batterlike dough that is dropped like a dumpling into boiling water. It is a traditional Umbrian dish from Gubbio and is usually served with finely shaved white truffles over the top. I added diced dried apricots when I made these the first time. This gave them a subtle, sweet flavor, and I dedicated the first bite to those inspirational women chefs at Le Noci (page 13). Serve these as a first course.*

Preheat the oven to 350° F.

Place the squash chunks in a casserole dish large enough to hold them in a single layer. Pour in ½ cup of water and cover the dish with a piece of aluminum foil. Bake the squash about 45 minutes, until a knife is inserted easily into a chunk.

Let the squash cool until it is easy to handle. Scrape and discard the seeds, then scoop the squash into a bowl and throw away the skins. Mash the squash with a fork to smooth it out. You will need 1½ cups to make the recipe. Stir in the flour, egg yolks, salt, cinnamon, apricots, and half of the cheese. Cover the bowl and refrigerate at least 2 hours or overnight. This will make it easier to handle.

Butter a casserole dish and set it aside. Bring a large pot of water to a boil.

Use 2 soup spoons to pick up some of the batter and drop it into the boiling water. Do not crowd the pot. Make 6 to 8 at a time. When they bob to the surface of the pot, scoop them out with a slotted spoon and transfer them to the casserole dish. Keep them covered and warm until all the batter is used.

Melt the butter in a small pot and pour it over the top of the gnocchi. Sprinkle the remaining cheese over the top and bake about 20-25 minutes, or until heated through. Plan on 4 or 5 as an individual serving.

# Biscotti by Any Other Name Are Still Cookies

*Biscottini di Vino Rosso* (Little Red Wine Cookies)

*Ciambellette* (Aniseed Ring Biscuits)

*Mezzalune* (Almond Crescent Cookies)

W hat's in a name? Of a *biscotto,* I mean. The names of Italian sweet nibbles read like a never-ending litany with some strange- and some endearing-sounding names like sweet mouthfuls, queen cookies, and bones of the dead. The universal word *biscotti* has come to mean cookies in general, but more specifically it is associated with the hard-as-a-rock variety that needs to be dunked into wine or coffee to soften them.

*A gift of Italian pastries, what could be better?*

Would it surprise you to know that biscotti are eaten for "breakfast"? I use the word loosely since most Italians do not eat breakfast as we know it—cereal, fruit, and toast, or eggs and bacon. Instead they munch on biscotti or a *cornetto* (croissant) washed down with a cappuccino at a nearby bar.

Some regions of Italy have a bigger sweet tooth than others when it comes to biscotti. Umbria does not. The variety of cookies is modest compared with other of regions such as Sicily and the Veneto. While I was in Umbria, I visited my share of *pasticcerie* to sample some of the confections of the region. One shop, Ceccarani di Santino on Piazza Matteotti in Perugia, has a wonderful array of biscotti from all over Italy. There are *baci di dama, taralli, stelle, ciambellette, tozzetti.* The list goes on. It is difficult to control one's urges in a place like this, so it is best to be dainty and ask the clerk for a small sampling of the shop's best sellers. These, I was told by Lara, the clerk behind the counter, are *mezzalune,* crescent-shaped cookies with finely ground nuts; *biscottini di vino* (little wine cookies), which should also not be missed; and *ciambellette,* the little ring-shaped cookies flavored with aniseeds.

She told me that schoolchildren come in to get these for their *merenda,* or afternoon snack. I was sold and asked for a sampling of each, which I devoured in no time. *"Buono?"* she asked, and I concurred, nodding, with cookie crumbs outlining my lips. I knew that when I got home I would want to re-create each of these treats for our television audience, who are always asking for more cookie recipes. Which goes to prove that the appeal of cookies or biscotti is universal.

# Biscottini di Vino Rosso

## Little Red Wine Cookies

Makes about 6 dozen

*Wine cookies exist for exactly what their name implies: dunking in wine. So they are popular during* vendemmia *(wine crush) season in Italy. It is best to chill the dough for at least two hours before forming it into small bagel-shaped cookies, which makes them rather* carino *(cute-looking). Red wine is used in the recipe, resulting in a lavender-colored dough, but white wine can also be used.*

*1 cup sugar*

*1 cup vegetable oil*

*1 cup dry red wine*

*4½ cups unbleached all-purpose flour*

*2 teaspoons baking powder*

*1 egg plus 1 tablespoon water, mixed together for egg wash*

In an electric mixer on medium speed, blend together the sugar, vegetable oil, and wine.

Sift the flour and baking powder together, then add them to the sugar mixture. Blend together on medium speed until a soft dough forms. The dough should not be sticky but soft and smooth.

Transfer the dough to a bowl. Cover the bowl tightly with plastic wrap and refrigerate for at least 2 hours or overnight. Once chilled, the dough is very easy to work with.

Preheat the oven to 350° F.

To form the cookies, break off small pieces and roll them with the palm of your hand to form a 4-inch rope that is ½ inch thick. Bring the ends together and pinch them tightly, forming a circle that looks like a miniature bagel. Place the cookies 1 inch apart on ungreased baking sheets. Brush the tops of each cookie with the egg wash.

Bake the cookies for 17 to 20 minutes, or until the tops are firm to the touch and the bottoms are golden brown. Remove to a cooling rack and cool completely. Store in airtight containers.

# Ciambellette

## Aniseed Ring Biscuits

Makes 4 dozen

5 large eggs

3 tablespoons
extra-virgin olive oil

1 tablespoon
grated lemon zest

1 teaspoon
vanilla extract

4 tablespoons sugar plus
extra for dipping the
rings before baking

2½ teaspoons aniseeds,
slightly crushed if
desired

2¾ to 3¼ cups
unbleached
all-purpose flour

¼ teaspoon salt

2 teaspoons
baking powder

*I could have eaten more than one of these at the Ceccarani di Santino pastry shop. These little rings with the flavor of licorice are a favorite of mine, and they freeze beautifully.*

In a mixing bowl, combine 4 eggs, olive oil, lemon zest, vanilla, sugar, and aniseeds.

On a sheet of waxed paper sift together 2¾ cups of flour, salt, and baking powder. Slowly add to the egg mixture and combine to make a smooth but fairly stiff dough. If more flour is needed, add it a little at a time until the right consistency is obtained. All the flour may not be necessary, depending on the type of flour used and the size of the eggs.

Divide the dough into 4 equal pieces. Work with 1 piece at a time and keep the remaining pieces covered so they do not dry out.

Roll each piece into a 12-inch-long rope and cut twelve 1-inch pieces from each rope. Bring the ends together to form a circle and pinch them closed.

Preheat the oven to 350° F. Line baking sheets with parchment paper.

Beat the remaining egg and 1 tablespoon of water lightly with a fork. Dip each ring into the egg wash and then in the sugar. Place the rings 1 inch apart on baking sheets.

Bake the *ciambellette* for 20 to 25 minutes, or just until they are golden brown. Cool on racks.

# Mezzalune

## Almond Crescent Cookies

Makes 2½ dozen

*Buttery, sandy, and biscuitlike are the words that come to mind when describing the wonderful taste and texture of these crescent-shaped almond cookies from Umbria that remind me of the Russian tea cakes my mother used to make at Christmastime. The secret to the texture of this cookie is to grind the almonds very fine, which is best done in a food processor. These are so delicate that care must be taken when removing the cookies from the baking sheet. This is where patience is definitely a virtue. Allow these to cool on the sheet for at least 10 minutes; otherwise, they will crumble. Use a gentle hand when coating them in confectioners' sugar.*

*1 cup (4 ounces) blanched, slivered almonds*

*½ cup sugar*

*2 cups unbleached all-purpose flour*

*¼ teaspoon salt*

*12 tablespoons (1½ sticks) unsalted butter, cut into bits*

*1 teaspoon almond extract*

*1 cup confectioners' sugar*

Preheat the oven to 325° F.

Line 2 baking sheets with parchment paper and set aside.

Grind the almonds with the sugar in a food processor until the almonds are the consistency of fine bread crumbs. Add the flour, salt, and butter, and pulse 2 or 3 times. With the motor running, add the almond extract and continue processing until the mixture begins to leave the sides of the bowl and forms a soft ball of dough.

Carefully remove the ball of dough from the bowl. Pinch off walnut-size pieces and roll them into 4-inch-long ropes the thickness of your middle finger. Form crescent or **c** shapes and place them on the baking sheets, spacing them about 1 inch apart.

Bake on the middle shelf of the oven for 20 minutes. When done they should be firm to the touch but not too brown. Allow the cookies to cool on the baking sheet to firm up.

Sift the confectioners' sugar into a 1-quart bowl. Roll the crescents in the sugar, coating them well.

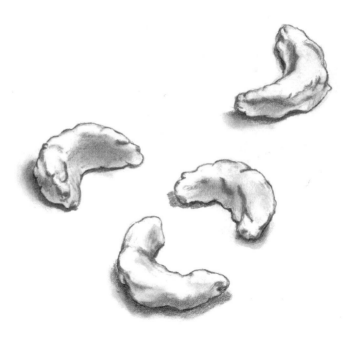

# City of Chocolate

*Spumone al Cioccolato* (Chocolate Spumone)

*Pere al Cioccolato* (Pears with Chocolate)

*I*t was worth making the drive through demolition-derby traffic to get to Eurochocolate, that sensational get-your-fix chocolate convention that takes place each October in the city of Perugia. Eurochocolate is an international confectionery show that attracts people from around the globe who want to delight in nibbles fashioned

*Two friends contemplate chocolate.*

into shapes that most of us can only fantasize about. Would you dare crack into Perugia's famous fountain, the Fontana Maggiore, made completely from chocolate? The Leaning Tower of Pisa? The Colosseum? Every conceivable form in milk, dark, and white chocolate is here. People packed as tightly as sardines line the expanse of the Corso Vannucci, eating their way down the corso and coming upon display after display, each one more elaborate than the last. There are fabulous window displays of chocolate as well—even an entire chocolate symphony orchestra! And visitors do not just reserve a room in any hotel; they request an early booking at the Etruscan Chocolate hotel in Via Campo di Marte where they eat, live, and sleep chocolate!

And if Eurochocolate were not enough to convince people of the virtues of chocolate, there is also the Compagnia del Cioccolato, a nonprofit group committed to seeing that chocolate is always manufactured according to rigid specifications and that its quality is never adulterated by artificial additives such as palm oil. Eating good-quality chocolate is one thing, but what about cooking with it? In my kitchen the same rules apply: Use the best quality you can find, and that means chocolate with a high ratio of butterfat.

Only one name synonymous with chocolate is revered in all of Italy, and that is Perugina; its major factory and chocolate museum are located in San Sisto, not far from the city center. Perugina chocolate was started by the Buitoni family, a company that makes commercially prepared dried pasta. Eventually Nestlé, the international corporate conglomerate, took over the business in order to satisfy a growing global craving for chocolate. Today it oversees the production of many types of Perugina confections, from the fantastic giant chocolate Easter eggs to the caramels to the nougat known as *torrone*. The most famous and most recognizable of its products, created in 1922, is Baci (kisses), those silver and blue foil–wrapped morsels of smooth, creamy chocolate encasing a delicious hazelnut. People refer to them as the "food of the gods," and they have become the edible logo of Perugina.

The Museo Storico Perugina (historic Perugina museum) adjacent to the factory showcases everything: the history of how cocoa beans arrived in Europe from the Americas; displays of antique candy-making apparatuses, old candy molds, and advertising posters that tell the story of Perugina's history; early television commercials for Perugina chocolate featuring Frank Sinatra; and letters and tributes from hundreds of famous people.

# Spumone al Cioccolato

## Chocolate Spumone

Serves 12

*Perugina semisweet chocolate is used in this recipe for* spumone, *a molded ice cream confection that is a refreshing end to a dinner party. Its name is derived from the word* spumare, *meaning foam. Make it ahead and freeze it. Team it with fresh raspberries or strawberries, or make a coulis, a fruit sauce to drizzle on the plate for an artistic presentation. It will look as though you have been in the kitchen all day!*

*7 ounces good-quality semisweet chocolate, coarsely chopped*

*3 tablespoons water*

*2 cups (1 pint) whipping cream*

*6 tablespoons sugar*

*3 egg yolks*

*2 ounces good-quality white chocolate, coarsely chopped*

Line a 10 × 4 × 2½-inch loaf pan or similar pan with plastic wrap, leaving a 1-inch overhang. Set aside.

Place the semisweet chocolate in a saucepan. Add the water and melt the chocolate over very low heat, stirring frequently until smooth. Set aside.

In a large bowl using an electric mixer, whip the cream with 2 tablespoons of the sugar until stiff. Set aside.

In another bowl, whip the egg yolks with the remaining sugar until the mixture is thick and lemon colored. Fold the egg mixture into the melted chocolate and then fold the chocolate mixture into the whipped cream along with the white chocolate. Spread the mixture evenly in the loaf pan and bring the overhanging plastic wrap over the top to cover the contents. Cover the top tightly with a sheet of aluminum foil. Freeze for at least 2 hours or up to 1 month. About 30 minutes before serving, remove the foil, unwrap the plastic wrap from the top, and unmold the spumone onto a decorative dish, gently pulling away the plastic wrap.

Use a knife dipped in ice water to make clean slices. For an elegant presentation cut the slices on the diagonal and stand the spumone on edge to create a vertical look. Serve as is or with chocolate sauce or a raspberry coulis (recipe follows).

## Raspberry Coulis

*½ pint raspberries, gently washed and dried*

*4 tablespoons sugar*

*1 teaspoon fresh lemon juice*

Puree the berries in a food processor or blender until very smooth. Strain the juice in a fine-mesh sieve over a bowl; discard the seeds and residue pulp.

Stir the sugar and lemon juice into the bowl with the raspberry puree. I store the sauce in plastic squeeze bottles and then decorate the plates of spumone just before serving.

Store the coulis in the refrigerator.

*Variation: Substitute 1½ cups fresh strawberries for the raspberries.*

# Pere al Cioccolato

## Pears with Chocolate

Serves 6

*Poached pears are fantastic for dessert, especially when they are covered in white and dark chocolate. These are a joy to make. I embellish the whole job by raining colored sprinkles over the finished pears to create a Joseph's Technicolor Dream Coat effect, then let my guests shatter them with a spoon. Pick pears with long stems for an attractive look—and to give you something to hang on to when painting them with chocolate.*

Peel and core the pears with an apple corer but leave them whole with the stems on. Cut a small slice off the bottom of each pear if necessary so they stay upright while cooking. Place the pears in a saucepan just large enough to accommodate them snugly. Pour in enough water to almost cover the pears. Add the sugar, cinnamon stick, and lemon juice. Simmer the pears gently for 20 to 25 minutes, or until a small knife can be inserted effortlessly into them. Do not overcook them to the point of being mushy. With a slotted spoon remove the pears to a dish to cool to room temperature.

To make the chocolate sauce: If using all semisweet chocolate, place it in a bowl set over warm, not hot, water. Stir in the vegetable oil and corn syrup to melt the ingredients slowly. The chocolate should be shiny and smooth.

If using white and dark chocolate, follow the above procedure but melt the chocolate in separate bowls using half of the vegetable oil and half of the corn syrup for each type.

*6 ripe but not mushy Bartlett, Bosc, or Anjou pears with nice stems*

*⅓ cup sugar*

*One 2-inch piece of cinnamon stick*

*2 tablespoons fresh lemon juice*

CHOCOLATE SAUCE

*1 cup chopped semisweet chocolate or ½ cup each semisweet and white chocolate*

*1 tablespoon vegetable oil*

*1 tablespoon corn syrup*

*Fresh mint leaves*

*Colored candy sprinkles*

*Strawberry coulis (see page 34) (optional)*

Hold the pears by the stem over the bowl. Working quickly, dip a fork in the warm chocolate and drizzle it over the tops of the pears. If using both chocolates, first drizzle the dark chocolate and let it dry a bit, then drizzle the white chocolate over the pears. Let the pears dry on waxed paper before placing them on serving dishes. Garnish with a mint leaf.

To cover the pears with candied sprinkles, paint the pears with the chocolate sauce using a pastry brush to cover them completely. While the glaze is still warm, sprinkle the pears with the candy sprinkles. This makes a really nice party look.

If you want to serve the pears without chocolate, make the strawberry coulis using the recipe on page 34. Pool some of the sauce around the bottom of each pear and garnish with a fresh mint leaf.

# Destination Deruta

*Ciaramicola* (Meringue Baked Sweet Bread)

*Crema Contadina* (Farmer-Style Pureed Bean Soup)

*Deruta pottery—beautiful, isn't it?*

$M$y kitchen is chock-full of it, but I cannot help myself. I love the artistic majolica (ceramic ware) of Deruta, a city about eight miles from Perugia that is the center for this craft in Umbria and known the world over. What makes Deruta so important in this trade is the lime-clay deposits found nearby that are the raw materials for the ceramic industry. The industry began in the thirteenth century and reached its glory in the sixteenth century as a result of the Salt War, when Deruta opposed the Pope and was plundered and destroyed. During the years of peace that followed, the art of working with clay became very popular. In the beginning, household objects such as pitchers, bowls, and basins were produced with very little decoration and in colors of green and brown. In the sixteenth century the choice of colors expanded to include orange, blue, and yellow, and the designs became more intricate—and today they include everything from geometric designs to floral, animals, grotesques, religious figures, noble coats of arms, mythological scenes, and ceremonial plates.

Most of Deruta's eight thousand residents are involved in the production of majolica. I am lucky to know some of the artists who design these ceramics, and I was glad when one of them, Franco Mari, whose pieces I have collected for years, was willing to let me see how the clay is fired and decorated. Via Tibernia, where his shop is located, is a ceramic lover's paradise: a dizzying street dedicated to shops of show-stopping, vibrant-colored ceramics that feature classic and modern designs.

Franco, a pleasant man, trains and oversees the artists who apply the colors to terra-cotta, and his energetic wife, Rita, who is thin enough to walk the runway of any fashion house, runs the day-to-day business of filling the hundreds of orders that come mostly from the United States. They are thrilled that they have so many American customers. Franco learned the business from his father and then went to art school to further develop his skills. I could sense his deep devotion to his work; each piece was like a precious child, and he talked fondly of them. He told me that his inspiration came not only from old classic Deruta designs but also from blending old designs with those that captured his imagination from American Indian designs of the southwest United States, namely Arizona and New Mexico.

I watched the rows of artists—some young, some old—carefully apply the colors, each in its specific place, and the individuality of this art was evident; no two pieces are exactly alike.

What I love most about Franco's ceramics is the shiny, smooth-as-silk, high-quality glaze that was the final step in finishing each piece. Once the glaze was applied, a kaleidoscope of colors popped out like a spilled box of crayons. I love to run my hands over the smooth surfaces. I can imagine a use for everything in Franco's shop. On a previous visit I spotted wonderful dishes with a stylized rooster design and decided on the spot that I needed a set of those dishes! I use them often, as well as the geometric-designed cake stand that is a regal resting place for the likes of airy sponge cakes, chocolate cakes, and all sorts of pastries. They look . . . well, so Italian when I display them! And I know this is silly, but espresso seems to taste better in Franco's sweet little espresso cups. Maybe it has something to do with the steam coming up from a tiny cup brimming with lots of colors. Besides, using the pieces is a wonderful reminder that Deruta is a ceramic lover's destination.

# *Ciaramicola*

## Meringue Baked Sweet Bread

Makes 2 loaves

*T*his unusual and fun-to-make yeast bread looks more like a rustic cake because of its baked meringue topping and covering of brightly colored sprinkles. It is part of an ancient Umbrian tradition that involves a young woman about to be married who presents this cake to her fiancé on Easter Sunday. Alkermes, the unusual ingredient that turns the crumb a soft pink hue, is a liqueur made from cinnamon, cloves, sugar, and cochineal, and it is said to have its beginnings in the Renaissance. Alkermes is available from Italian specialty shops (see Mail Order Sources, page 199). Use cranberry liqueur as a substitute.

    I serve this bread on a footed Deruta cake dish.

I make this dough in a stand mixer, but you can also do it by hand in a large bowl. Dissolve the yeast in the buttermilk and stir in 1 teaspoon of the sugar. Allow the mixture to sit about 5 minutes. On low speed with the paddle attachment, beat in the eggs 1 at a time until well blended. Beat in the zest, butter, Alkermes, salt, and the remaining sugar until a smooth mixture is obtained. Slowly beat in the flour, 1 cup at a time, until a ball of dough forms and leaves the sides of the bowl. The dough should feel soft and just slightly tacky on your hands. Remove the dough from the bowl to a work surface lightly sprinkled with flour. Knead the dough with your hands into a smooth, soft ball. Place the dough in a bowl and cover tightly with plastic wrap. Let the dough rise about 2 hours, or until it has doubled in size.

1 tablespoon
  active dry yeast

1¼ cups buttermilk,
  heated to 110° F

¼ cup plus 1 teaspoon
  sugar

3 large eggs at
  room temperature

Grated zest of
  1 large orange

4 tablespoons
  unsalted butter
  at room temperature

½ cup Alkermes or
  cranberry liqueur

1 teaspoon salt

5 to 5¼ cups unbleached
  all-purpose flour

## MERINGUE TOPPING

*4 large egg whites
at room temperature*

*¼ teaspoon salt*

*¼ cup sugar*

*Colored candy sprinkles*

When the dough has risen, punch it down and knead it with your hands for 3 or 4 minutes. It should feel soft and not stick to your hands or the board. If you need more flour, add it 1 tablespoon at a time until the dough is the right consistency. Be careful not to add too much flour or the bread will have too tight a crumb and be dry.

Preheat the oven to 375° F. Position the oven rack on the middle shelf. Line 2 baking sheets with parchment paper and set aside.

Divide the dough in half and work with one half at a time.

Roll the dough out on a lightly floured surface into a 26-inch-long rope. Cut 4 inches off the rope and set aside.

Bring the 2 ends of the rope together to form a ring and place it on a baking sheet. Cut the 4-inch piece in half and roll each piece into a 7-inch rope; make a cross with the 2 pieces of dough over the top of the circle. Ironically, you will not see the cross on the bread once it is covered in meringue, but this is part of the symbolism of Easter. Cover the dough and allow it to rise for 30 minutes.

Bake the dough for 30 minutes, or until it is almost done; insert a cake skewer into the dough to see if it is baked through.

Meanwhile, prepare the meringue topping: Beat the egg whites on medium speed until foamy. Add the salt, raise the speed to high, and add the sugar in a steady stream, beating until the egg whites are fluffy and hold their peaks.

Remove the baking sheet from the oven and, working quickly, use a rubber spatula to spread half of the meringue over the top and sides of the bread. Sprinkle the colored candies over the top and sides and return the bread to the oven. Bake 10 minutes more, or until the meringue is nicely browned. Remove the bread from the oven and allow to cool completely.

Repeat the process with the remaining dough. You may need to rewhip the remaining meringue just before spreading it on the second loaf.

This bread is best eaten the day it is made but will keep a day or two in the refrigerator, although the meringue may soften and settle a bit.

Cut into thick slices for serving.

# *Crema Contadina*

## Farmer-Style Pureed Bean Soup

Makes about 2 quarts

*Serve this nutritious and filling pureed soup, made from dried red kidney beans, carrots, celery, onion, and rosemary, in your most elegant soup tureen. These humble ingredients create a rich flavor, another good example of the simplicity of Umbrian cooking. Try making it with a variety of dried beans such as cannellini, chickpea, and cranberry. Soak the beans overnight to cut down on the cooking time.*

Soak the beans overnight in cold water.

Drain the beans and place them in a soup pot with the carrots, onion, celery, scallions, olive oil, and rosemary. Add the chicken broth. Bring the ingredients to a boil, then lower the heat and cook, covered, until the beans are tender and the skin easily slips off the beans. This will take about 50 minutes.

Puree the soup in batches in a food processor or blender until smooth. Transfer the soup to a soup pot and season with salt and pepper to taste. Reheat the mixture until hot, then pour into a soup tureen or ladle from the pot into soup bowls. Top with a few onion slices and pass extra olive oil to drizzle on top of the soup.

**1½ cups dried red kidney beans or a combination of dried beans**

**2 carrots, scraped and cut into quarters**

**1 medium yellow onion, peeled and quartered**

**2 ribs celery with leaves, quartered**

**6 scallions, green tops only, cut into quarters**

**3 tablespoons olive oil plus more for serving**

**1 large sprig rosemary, needles only**

**8 cups chicken broth**

**¼ teaspoon salt**

**Freshly ground coarse black pepper**

**1 thinly sliced red onion for garnish**

# In Search of Black Celery

*Insalata di Melanzane Grigliata* (Grilled Eggplant Salad)

*Scafata* (Fava Bean Casserole)

*Sedano Nero Ripieno con Salsiccia* (Pork-Stuffed Celery)

*Parmigiana di Cipolla di Cannara* (Layered Onion Casserole from Cannara)

*Terrina di Verza* (Stuffed Cabbage Cooked in Earthenware)

*I*t seemed like a culinary contradiction to me. Black celery? Isn't all celery green? Apparently not in Trevi, a small hill town in southeastern Umbria famous for *sedano nero* (black celery) as well as for its fine production of extra-virgin olive oil from the moraiolo olive, which also earns Trevi the title of the "city of oil."

I was more than curious about any vegetable that is black, so on the way to Lizori to cook with chef Daniela Bottoni (see page 81), I stopped in Trevi, hoping that it would be available in the local market. Trevi's main square is quaint and small with a few shops. A sign over one said *frutta e verdure* (fruit and vegetables), and it had crates of figs, oranges, berries, eggplant, fava beans, sturdy heads of cabbage, and plump onions sitting prettily just outside the entrance. I was tempted to buy them to make some of my favorite Umbrian vegetable dishes, including *scafata* (fava bean casserole), grilled eggplant, and an onion casserole that I had in nearby Cannara, the onion capital of Italy.

Surely they must have black celery as well, though I did wonder why it was not displayed with the rest of the vegetables. I parted the colorful rope curtains framing the doorway to the store and stepped inside.

*"Buon giorno,"* I said, introducing myself to a woman sitting at the checkout counter. Her name was Marcella. *"Avete sedano nero?"* Do you have black celery? *"Si, certo, signora, guarda qua."* She took me by the hand, led me to the back of the store, and pointed to wooden boxes filled with gorgeous celery that was as white as could be at the base and had dramatic dark green stalks and even darker green leaves. *"Ma perchè non è nero?"* Why isn't it black? I asked. I

could see that she was settling into a long explanation, so I took out my notebook and hung on her every word.

*Sedano nero* is planted in very limited quantities beginning in March and April, and is harvested in October. It is cultivated in a narrow zone of land between Borgo and the Clitunno River where the ground is damp and fertile. She pointed to the celery tops. The celery must be watched carefully to know when it is ready to be harvested. The leaves must be dark green, almost black, and this is where *sedano nero* gets its name. But if the celery is left to grow without proper care taken for its watering and for the fertilizing of the soil, it can become very woody. Now I was beginning to get the picture. She went on to explain that this celery was unique not only for its color but also for its intense taste and delicate nonfibrous texture. To achieve this the farmer mounds rich soil around the base of the plant to prevent the formation of tough fibers and to keep the bulbous part white.

The economy and gastronomy of Trevi are based on the production of black celery, extra-virgin olive oil, and the locally made sausages that, Marcella explained, are always in high demand. Black celery is so revered in Trevi that each year on the third Sunday in October the *Sagra del Sedano e Della Salsiccia* (Festival of Celery and Sausage) takes place: The townspeople come together to celebrate the harvest and enjoy such dishes as *pinzimonio,* bowls of extra-virgin olive oil flavored with salt and pepper in which stalks of *sedano nero* are dipped and eaten raw. Celery stuffed with local sausage and fried in a batter is also a specialty (see the recipe on page 51).

I was so glad I took that detour to Trevi to learn all this that I almost forgot about my appointment to cook with Daniela in Lizori! I thanked Marcella profusely, and as I was leaving, she handed me a bouquet of *sedano nero*! I am a believer.

# *Insalata di Melanzane Grigliata*

## Grilled Eggplant Salad

Serves 6 to 8

*A*lla griglia *(on the grill) defines much of the cooking of Umbria, right down to its vegetables. It is such an effortless way to prepare them, and I love how delicious they taste with a little charring. Add a drizzle of Umbrian extra-virgin olive oil and a little salt, and you've come as near to perfection as you can. In the summer I have loads of eggplant from the garden, but produce markets make it available year-round, so it's easy to enjoy this refreshing salad made with grilled eggplant.*

Heat the oven to 350° F. Preheat the grill.

Spread the pine nuts on a small baking sheet and toast for 4 to 5 minutes. Do not let them burn. Transfer to a dish to cool.

Lightly brush the eggplant slices with olive oil on both sides. Place them on the hot grill and turn them frequently until they start to brown and take on grill marks. Transfer them to a dish large enough to hold them in 1 layer.

Make the dressing in a bowl by whisking together the olive oil, shallots, parsley, vinegar, salt, pepper, and mint. Pour over the eggplant, cover, and marinate several hours at room temperature. Just before serving, sprinkle on the pine nuts and cheese.

**¼ cup pine nuts**

**2 medium eggplant, washed, dried, stems removed, and cut into ¼-inch-thick lengthwise slices**

**¾ cup extra-virgin olive oil plus more for brushing on eggplants**

**3 shallots, peeled and thinly sliced**

**⅓ cup minced Italian parsley**

**4 tablespoons white wine vinegar**

**¾ teaspoon salt**

**Freshly ground black pepper to taste**

**¼ cup minced mint**

**4 ounces sweet Gorgonzola or feta cheese, crumbled**

# Scafata

## Fava Bean Casserole

Serves 4 to 6

*1 cup shelled fava beans
(about 2 pounds
unhulled) or lima
beans*

*¼ cup extra-virgin
olive oil*

*1 medium onion, peeled
and coarsely chopped*

*1 stalk celery, chopped*

*1 carrot, chopped*

*1 pound Swiss chard,
stemmed, washed,
and torn into pieces*

*1 pound plum tomatoes,
cored, seeded, and cut
into coarse pieces*

*½ teaspoon fine sea salt*

*Freshly ground coarse
black pepper to taste*

*½ cup diced oil-cured
black olives*

Scafata *means hull, and in this recipe it refers to hulling or removing the outer skin of fresh fava beans. Doing this reveals a creamy bean similar in appearance to fresh lima beans. If your fava beans are small, this step can be eliminated. In this typical Umbrian recipe, fava beans are cooked with Swiss chard and fresh tomatoes for an unpretentious, nutrition-packed dish.*

Place the fava beans in a saucepan, cover with water, and boil about 6 minutes, or just until the outer skin slips away easily from the bean (if they are large) when pressed between your fingers; otherwise, cook the beans about 4 minutes. Drain and refresh them under cold water. If the beans are large, remove the outer skin. Set the beans aside.

Heat the olive oil in a 12- or 14-inch sauté pan. Stir in the onion, celery, and carrot, and cook until the vegetables begin to soften. Stir in the fava beans and Swiss chard. Cover the pan and allow the mixture to simmer for 20 minutes. Uncover and stir in the tomatoes. Cover and cook 5 minutes more. Off the heat, stir in the salt, pepper, and olives.

Serve hot as a vegetable side dish or a luncheon dish accompanied by good coarse bread.

# Sedano Nero Ripieno con Salsiccia

## Pork-Stuffed Celery

Serves 8

*This dish of sweet pork sausage stuffed with "black" celery, known as sedano nero ripieno, is celebrated in Trevi every October as part of the Sagra del Sedano e Della Salsiccia (Festival of Celery and Sausage). The dish was tested with regular celery from the grocery store, and there were no complaints at the dinner table. Use the largest stalks you can find. There are three separate steps to the recipe—filling, frying, and baking. To ease the preparation, make the sauce and batter one day, and fill and bake the celery the next.*

To make the batter: Whisk the flour and milk together in a bowl until smooth. Cover and let thicken for several hours. Or make the batter ahead and refrigerate overnight.

To make the sauce: Use a chef's knife and coarsely chop the onion, celery, and carrot together. Heat the olive oil in a saucepan until it begins to shimmer. Add the minced vegetables and cook over low heat until they are soft. Stir in the red pepper flakes and cook 1 minute more. Stir in the tomatoes, wine, and salt. Cover the pan, lower the heat, and simmer for 30 minutes. The sauce can be made several days ahead.

For the filling: Divide the sausage among the celery stalks, stuffing it into the cavity of each piece. Be sure to press it in well.

Preheat the oven to 350° F.

Have ready a baking sheet lined with paper towels.

Heat the vegetable oil in a sauté pan until it is 375° F. Use a ther-

### BATTER

**½ cup unbleached all-purpose flour**

**1 cup whole milk**

### SAUCE

**1 small onion, peeled and quartered**

**1 stalk celery, quartered**

**1 carrot, scraped and quartered**

**2 tablespoons extra-virgin olive oil**

**¼ teaspoon red pepper flakes**

**1¾ pounds plum tomatoes, fresh or canned, coarsely chopped**

**½ cup dry red wine**

**Sea salt to taste**

*1 pound sweet Italian
pork sausages,
casings removed*

*8 large stalks celery,
washed, dried, and
trimmed, and stalks
cut in half widthwise*

*1 cup vegetable oil*

*½ cup grated
Parmigiano-Reggiano
cheese*

*¼ cup grated
pecorino cheese*

mometer to gauge the temperature or drop a small amount of batter into the pan; if it browns immediately, the oil is hot enough.

Pour the batter into a shallow bowl. Coat each celery-stuffed piece with the batter and fry quickly in the oil, a few at a time, turning the pieces once. Cook just until the sausage turns gray. Transfer the celery to the paper towels to drain.

Layer the celery in each of two 9 × 12-inch baking dishes. Divide the sauce between the 2 dishes, spooning it evenly over the top of the celery.

Divide the cheeses and sprinkle over the top of each dish.

Cover the dishes with foil and bake for 45 to 50 minutes, or just until the celery is tender. Serve hot with some of the juices from the dish.

# Parmigiana di Cipolla di Cannara

## Layered Onion Casserole from Cannara

Serves 6 to 8

*Cannara, a small town near the ceramic center of Deruta, is known as the onion capital of Italy, and many traditional dishes from antipasto to main courses feature the humble onion as the central ingredient. So revered are the onions of Cannara that every September La Festa della Cipolla (The Onion Festival) is held, and visitors can get their fill of all sorts of delicious onion dishes. My favorite is this exquisite fried onion and ragù casserole laced with a velvety cream sauce. The dish should be prepared in stages to make the final assembly easy. I make the cream sauce and the ragù several days ahead and refrigerate them. The onions are cooked just before the final assembly. Use the ragù sauce on page 141 for this recipe.*

Follow the directions for making the *ragù* and set aside if assembling the dish that day or refrigerate the *ragù* for up to 5 days for later assembly.

To make the cream sauce: Melt the butter in a 2-quart saucepan over medium heat. Stir in the flour and cook until the mixture is smooth but not browned. Slowly pour in the milk and continue to cook, stirring frequently, until the sauce thickens enough to coat the back of a spoon. Remove from the heat and stir in the salt and nutmeg. Cover the pot and set aside or refrigerate the sauce if you are planning to make the casserole a few days later.

Have ready 2 baking sheets lined with paper towels.

**Ragù Umbro *(page 141)***

CREAM SAUCE

**4 tablespoons unsalted butter**

**¼ cup flour**

**4 cups milk**

**1 teaspoon salt**

**¼ teaspoon freshly ground nutmeg**

FILLING

**2 pounds Spanish onions, peeled and cut into ¼-inch-thick rings**

**5 tablespoons flour**

**1 to 1½ cups vegetable oil**

**8 ounces mozzarella cheese, diced**

**6 tablespoons grated Parmigiano-Reggiano cheese**

Place the onion rings in a large paper bag with the flour. Close the bag and shake it to lightly coat the rings.

Heat 1 cup of vegetable oil in a heavy-duty pot or sauté pan. When the oil begins to shimmer, add the onions in batches and brown on both sides. As they brown, remove them to the paper-lined baking sheets. Add more oil as needed to cook all the onions.

Preheat the oven to 350° F.

Spread ½ cup of cream sauce in the bottom of a 13 × 8¼ × 2-inch casserole or similar dish.

Spread 2 cups of *ragù* over the cream sauce. Spread one-third of the onions over the *ragù,* one-third of the mozzarella over the onions, ½ cup of cream sauce over the mozzarella, and 2 table-spoons of Parmigiano-Reggiano over the mozzarella. Continue, making 2 more layers in the same manner. Pour the remaining cream sauce over the casserole.

Bake, uncovered, for 30 to 35 minutes, or until it is bubbly and hot. Serve immediately.

# Terrina di Verza

## Stuffed Cabbage Cooked in Earthenware

*green salad*
*cheese & pears*

Serves 4

*One of my favorite restaurants in Umbria is Villa Roncalli in the town of Foligno. This well-appointed country restaurant specializes in spit-roasted meats, game, fowl . . . and songbirds. Since my last visit there, the Italian government, along with nature lovers, has taken steps to protect the depleting songbird population, and they are no longer featured on the menu. One of the dishes I recall with fondness and make often is* terrina di verza, *or stuffed Savoy cabbage rolls. They are juicy and flavorful, with a wonderful lemon taste, and a good example of rustic country cooking. They are usually cooked in earthenware, which keeps in the heat and makes the rolls juicy, but I use a heavy-duty oven casserole and have great success.*

Fill a large pot with water and bring to a boil. Add the cabbage and cook just until the leaves begin to wilt and are limp enough for rolling. Remove the cabbage with a slotted spoon and allow to cool until easy to handle.

Heat the olive oil in a sauté pan, and when it is hot, add the meats and garlic. Cook until the meats are browned, then drain in a colander to remove the excess fat. Transfer the meats to a bowl and stir in the parsley, marjoram or thyme, lemon zest, bread crumbs, 2 tablespoons of the Parmigiano-Reggiano, all of the pecorino, the egg, salt, and pepper. Set the mixture aside.

Preheat the oven to 350° F.

Separate the cabbage leaves, keeping them as whole as possible.

- 1 medium head Savoy cabbage, washed and center core removed
- 2 tablespoons extra-virgin olive oil
- 8 ounces ground pork
- 4 ounces ground sirloin tips
- 4 ounces chicken breast
- 1 large clove garlic, minced
- ⅓ cup minced Italian parsley
- 2 teaspoons fresh minced marjoram or thyme, or ¼ teaspoon dried marjoram or thyme
- 1 tablespoon grated lemon zest
- ¼ cup fresh bread crumbs
- 6 tablespoons grated Parmigiano-Reggiano cheese

*2 tablespoons grated*
*pecorino cheese*

*1 egg, lightly beaten*

*1 teaspoon fine sea salt*

*Freshly ground coarse*
*black pepper*

*⅔ cup chicken broth*

If you need to patch, overlap the leaves. Divide the meat mixture among 8 of the largest leaves and roll each one up like a little bundle.

Lightly brush an earthenware baking dish or other casserole dish with oil and place the cabbage rolls in the dish. Pour the chicken broth around the rolls, cover the dish with aluminum foil, and bake for 30 minutes. Remove the foil, sprinkle the tops of the rolls with the remaining Parmigiano-Reggiano, and continue cooking the rolls 10 minutes more.

Serve the rolls hot with some of the juices poured over them.

*Variation: Five minutes before the rolls are done, add bits of sun-dried tomatoes.*

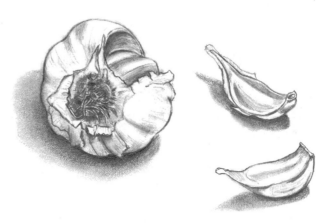

# La Cucina di Francesca

*Pappardelle* (Wide Ribbon Noodles)

*Faraona Arrosta* (Roasted Guinea Hen)

*Fave con Aglio e Pecorino* (Fava Beans with Olive Oil and Pecorino Cheese)

*Tarlo d'Aglio* (Wild Garlic Sauce)

*Cavallucci* (Horsemen's Cookies)

*Tozzetti Pasticceria Polticchia* (Cookies from the Polticchia Pastry Shop)

*Perfect pasta comes from experienced hands.*

*B*evagna is not to be missed. A little snip of a town near the wine center of Montefalco, it still retains its medieval look with its mellow brown stone gates, narrow streets, and beautiful piazza built in the twelfth and thirteenth centuries. And lonestanding Roman columns give evidence to its ancient history.

Bevagna is known for its handcrafts and for centuries was an important tile- and cloth-making center. Today it continues the tradition of rope- and basket-making, and prized workmanship in wrought iron. Every year toward the end of June Bevagna celebrates its most important festival: the *Mercato delle Gaite* (Market of Gaite). For a week the town becomes a medieval marketplace. Its citizens wear period costumes and practice old trades: The bakers make bread in open ovens; the basket makers create intricate containers from willow branches; the rope makers turn hemp into cords and ropes; and the taverns serve food prepared from antique recipes.

And amid all this charm and history lives Francesca Margutti, an accomplished cook, to whose home I was headed for lunch, thanks to a mutual friend, Analita Polticchia.

Analita's family owns a *pasticceria* in Bevagna and knows everyone. Her family has been in the pastry business since 1967, when her father, Luciano Polticchia, after years of experience in the pastry business with his brothers, decided to move with his family to the medieval town of Bevagna, open his own shop, and continue his passion for making breads and pastries. Everything made there is based on the use of pure and genuine ingredients. The breads, biscotti, and other pastries are well known, artisanal in nature, and reflect the antique recipes of the area. The jam tarts, *rocciata* (a strudel-like pastry filled with prunes, nuts, and spices), and *pancaciato* (cheese bread) are irresistible. The Polticchia family's simple and genuine creed is to pass their art on to generation after generation. Because Analita knew how interested I am in Umbrian cuisine, she wanted me to meet Francesca, who was going to demonstrate some classic Umbrian dishes for our television audience.

Meeting her in her cheery lime-green-painted kitchen, I was immediately comfortable in the lush surroundings of potted herbs, beautiful roses, cream-colored lilies, and intoxicating lavender plants that soaked up the noontime sun on the outdoor terrace. Francesca is a vigorous woman with short dark hair and a wide smile. It was evident from observing her efficiency in the kitchen that she had been making good food since she was a young girl.

But before the demonstration there was lunch to consider, and we were ushered outside to the terrace where a pristine table had been laid, starting with an antipasto of fresh fava beans, dressed in fragrant, deep-green-hued Umbrian extra-virgin olive oil, and pecorino cheese. There were perfumy, juicy melon slices, the perfect bed for see-through slices of prosciutto; there was a plate of attractively arranged spicy *salame locale,* dried tomatoes glistening in extra-virgin olive oil, and, of course good rustic bread. That would have been enough, but it would not have been Italian hospitality at its finest. Fresh, delicate ribbons of fettuccine followed with a sauce of wild garlic tops, cherry tomatoes, and dried red pepper flakes. I did not leave a trace on my plate. Next, an exquisitely prepared *faraona,* or guinea hen, seasoned with a mixture of herbs and cooked with wine, left me in awe, and I wondered how I would ever get through the afternoon as the wine flowed freely to accompany this *pranzo*. A plate of *cavallucci* and *tozzetti* cookies from Analita's *pasticceria* ended the meal, and we clapped fervently for this beautifully executed lunch.

Now it was show time, and Francesca had everything she needed to make pasta lined up on her wooden board; there was her wooden *matterello*—a rolling pin as long as a broom handle—along with fresh eggs in a large bowl and flour. Where was the salt? No salt until it was time to cook the pasta; then it was added to the cooking water, she explained.

I have made pasta hundreds of times, but watching Francesca make it was almost hypnotic as she whipped the eggs around with her hands in a fountain of flour. I timed her and found that it took three minutes for her to be happy with the look of the beaten eggs. She blended the flour into the eggs and used every bit of it, leaving not a speck on the board. Now that was planning! She kneaded the dough while telling us that she was going to cut it into *pappardelle*, those wide ribbons of noodles that go so well with wild hare or boar. I loved the way she rolled the dough onto the *matterello*, wrapping it around the pin and then unwrapping it in such a swift motion that the dough gave a rhythmic slapping sound against the wood.

When Francesca was satisfied that the dough was thin enough, she rolled it up gently like a jelly roll and cut it into half-inch-wide noodles and shook the rolls out to uncoil them. These silky yellow ribbons were perfect, and the smile on her face as she looked into the camera was her own stamp of approval that here in her cozy kitchen she had once again made perfect pasta, the badge of honor for any cook. *Basta!*

# *Pappardelle*

## Wide Ribbon Noodles

Makes about 1¼ pounds, enough to serve 6 to 8

*3 cups unbleached all-purpose flour*

*4 large eggs*

*Francesca Margutti made these wide ribbons of noodles called* pappardelle *with ease and precision, beating the eggs with her fingers for what seemed like an eternity. When I asked her what kind of sauce she would use with it, she suggested a choice of hare sauce, mushroom sauce, or black truffle sauce.* Pappardelle *means to gorge, and these are so light in texture that it is conceivable too many could be consumed with no difficulty at all. Use this recipe as the master to make other types of fresh cuts, including spaghetti, fettuccine, and lasagne noodles. Add a pinch of salt to the flour.*

Dump the flour in a heap on a work surface and use your hands to make a fountain, or *fontana* as Italian cooks call it. Crack the eggs into the center and use your hands to whip them around to break them up. Francesca did this for a full 3 minutes.

Begin bringing some of the flour from the inside of the fountain into the center, mixing it with the eggs. Continue like this until enough of the flour has been added to make a rough-looking ball of dough. Push the excess flour aside and knead the dough until it becomes smooth and has no bumpy spots, and it is not sticking to your hands. The dough should feel soft; adding too much flour will produce a dry dough.

Form the dough into a ball and place it on a lightly floured surface. Put a bowl over the top of it and allow it to rest about 30 minutes. This will help to relax the gluten in the dough and make it easier for you to roll out.

Cut the dough into thirds and work with one piece at a time; keep the remaining pieces covered so they do not dry out.

Use a rolling pin to roll the pieces out on a lightly floured surface into a 14 × 16-inch rectangle that is about 1/16 inch thick. I use a pastry wheel to cut 1/2-inch-wide strips to make the *pappardelle*. After cutting them, I put them on clean towels to dry or to hold until I am ready to cook them. Francesca rolls the sheets of dough up into a loose roll and then uses a knife to cut the noodles. Use whatever method works best for you.

To cook *pappardelle* or any other fresh pasta, start with a large pot of boiling water; at least 4 to 6 quarts of water is my rule. In Umbria the salt is added to the cooking water and not to the dough. Add 1 tablespoon of salt to the boiling water for every pound of pasta. Add the *pappardelle*. Remember that fresh pasta cooks in no time at all and should be *al dente,* meaning it should be firm, not mushy, but cooked through. Cook the *pappardelle* no longer than 3 or 4 minutes. Drain it in a colander and toss with your favorite sauce.

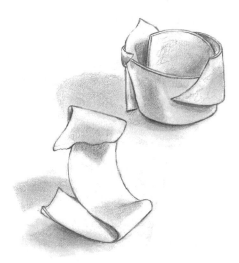

# *Faraona Arrosta*

## Roasted Guinea Hen

Serves 4

One 3½-pound
guinea hen, chicken,
or pheasant,
washed and dried

Sea salt

Freshly ground
coarse black pepper

3 tablespoons
extra-virgin olive oil

1 whole lemon

4 fresh sage leaves,
minced

4 tablespoons freshly
squeezed lemon juice

½ cup dry white wine

*Francesca Margutti made this moist, roasted faraona (guinea hen) for the secondo, or second course, of our lunch. Faraona actually translates to "pharaoh's hen," because these delicate birds were originally thought to come from Egypt. The taste is somewhere between chicken and pheasant. Simply prepared with herbs, fresh lemon juice, and a brushing of extra-virgin olive oil, they were so delicious that I had to control myself from licking my fingers at Francesca's table. It was one of the finest fowls I had ever eaten. I realize that guinea hen may not be easy to come by for everyone; in that case, try this recipe with chicken or pheasant.*

Preheat the oven to 350° F.

Rub the bird all over with salt and pepper. Brush the entire bird with the olive oil. Use a skewer to poke holes all over the lemon, then insert it into the cavity of the bird along with the minced sage leaves.

Place the bird on a roasting rack in a roasting pan and pop it into the oven. Allow it to cook for 30 minutes. Meanwhile, mix together the lemon juice and wine. Baste the bird with the mixture every 10 minutes until the bird is cooked through; this should take about 1 hour and 10 minutes, or until a meat thermometer inserted in the thickest part of the bird registers 185° F.

Transfer the bird to a cutting board. Remove the lemon from the cavity and discard it. Cut the bird into serving pieces and place them on a platter. Pour the pan drippings over the pieces and serve immediately.

# *Fave con Aglio e Pecorino*

## Fava Beans with Olive Oil and Pecorino Cheese

Serves 4 to 6

*That gleaming bowl of fresh fava beans dressed with Umbrian extra-virgin olive oil was a favorite of mine at Francesca Margutti's lunch. Fresh favas appear in late spring and last into early summer. Some markets carry frozen favas, but if you cannot find them, use lima beans—not quite the same thing, but good nonetheless. If the fava beans are large, the outer skin will need to be slipped off after they are cooked. Skip this step if the beans are small. Be sure to use a good-quality extra-virgin olive oil. If you can find Umbrian olive oil (see Mail Order Sources, page 199), this dish will have a slight spiciness to it.*

**3 pounds fresh fava beans, shelled (about 3 cups)**

**½ cup extra-virgin olive oil**

**Fine sea salt to taste**

**Freshly ground coarse black pepper to taste**

**1 cup coarsely grated Parmigiano-Reggiano cheese**

Pour the beans into a 2-quart saucepan and cover with cold water. Bring the beans to a boil and cook until a knife is inserted easily into them. Larger beans are cooked when the outer skins slip off easily when squeezed between your fingers. Do not overcook the beans; they should retain a bit of firmness. Drain the beans.

Pour the olive oil into a medium-size bowl and toss the beans in the oil to coat them. Sprinkle in the salt, pepper, and cheese. Toss again. Serve the beans warm or at room temperature.

# Tarlo d'Aglio

## Wild Garlic Sauce

½ cup extra-virgin
olive oil

1½ cups wild garlic tops
cut into 1-inch pieces

1 teaspoon dried
red pepper flakes

3 cups cherry tomatoes,
halved

Sea salt

Freshly ground coarse
black pepper to taste

1 pound fettuccine

*I could not get enough of this simple wild garlic sauce served over fettuccine. Wild garlic is available in the spring, but if it's not available, use wild leek tops, sometimes referred to as ramps, or wild onion tops. Spring onion tops are another possibility. The sauce is enough for 1 pound of fettuccine, either homemade or store-bought. The recipe is sufficient to feed four really hungry adults or six more moderate eaters. Either way, this dish is a winner.*

Heat the olive oil in a sauté pan. Add the garlic tops and cook for 4 or 5 minutes, just until they begin to wilt. Stir in the red pepper flakes and cook for 1 minute. Stir in the tomatoes, salt to taste, and pepper, and simmer, covered, for 10 minutes.

While the sauce simmers, cook the fettuccine in 4 quarts of boiling water to which 1 tablespoon of salt has been added. Cook until *al dente*, then drain and mix with the sauce.

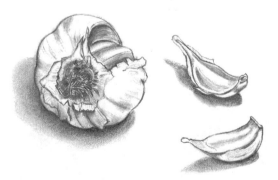

# *Cavallucci*

## Horsemen's Cookies

Makes about 4½ dozen

Cavallucci– *"little horses" or "horsemen's cookies"*– *have been made in many regions of Italy since medieval times, and the tradition continues at Pasticceria Polticchia in Bevagna. They get their name from horsemen who used to stop on their long journeys at* osterie *(inns and bars) to quench their thirst and eat* cavallucci *(which supposedly made them more thirsty, and that was good for the innkeeper). Some even say that the cookie's name was derived from the imprint of a horse that was stamped on top of each cookie. Surprisingly,* cavallucci *are shaped in a myriad of ways, some in a horseshoe and others in small squares; there is no standard shape. The dough is made very quickly in a saucepan on the stovetop and is thick and pastelike. You have to work quickly to mix the ingredients, so have everything measured out, ready to pour into the pan. These spicy, chewy morsels have a long shelf life because of all the spices.*

**3 cups unbleached all-purpose flour**

**2½ teaspoons baking powder**

**1½ cups water**

**1½ cups sugar**

**1 cup chopped walnuts**

**Grated zest of 2 large oranges**

**2 teaspoons ground cinnamon**

**1 teaspoon cloves**

**1½ teaspoons aniseeds, crushed**

**1 teaspoon anise flavoring**

Preheat the oven to 350° F.

Lightly grease a baking sheet and set it aside.

Sift the flour with the baking powder on a sheet of waxed paper and set it aside. This will make it easier to get it into the pan.

Mix the water and sugar together in a 2-quart saucepan. Bring to a boil, stirring constantly. Watch carefully because you do not want the mixture to boil too long—only until a little of the mixture dropped into a glass of water forms a ball. Stir in the nuts, zest, cinnamon, cloves, aniseeds, and flavoring. Off the heat stir in the flour mixture and mix until all the ingredients are combined. The dough will be sticky and thick. Scrape the dough out onto the baking sheet and use a rubber spatula to spread it into a 10 × 11-inch rectangle: or wet your hands and pat it into a rectangle.

Bake the dough for 15 minutes, or until it is firm to the touch and lightly browned around the edges. Cool the dough on a wire rack for 20 minutes. Cut it into squares or rectangles.

*Variation: Add ½ cup of candied orange or lemon peel to the mixture.*

# Tozzetti Pasticceria Polticchia

## Cookies from the Polticchia Pastry Shop

Makes 3 dozen

Tozzetti *means small morsels or bits, but it also refers to these heir-loom cookies made in Bevagna at Pasticceria Polticchia. My friend Analita Polticchia brought them to the lunch that I enjoyed at Francesca Margutti's house. The cookies look like biscotti and are airy and dry since there is no butter in the dough. Make them bite-size or larger.*

Tozzetti *store beautifully if well wrapped and kept in airtight tins, or you can freeze them for up to six months.*

3¼ cups unbleached all-purpose flour

1 cup sugar

½ teaspoon salt

2 tablespoons baking powder

6 eggs

1 teaspoon almond extract

1¼ cups sliced almonds

Measure the flour into a bowl. Stir in the sugar, salt, and baking powder. Set aside.

In another bowl, lightly beat the eggs with a wire whisk until frothy. Stir in the almond extract.

Combine the flour and egg mixtures. Stir in the nuts and mix the ingredients until well blended. The cookie dough will be soft. Cover the bowl with a piece of plastic wrap and refrigerate for several hours to make it easier to work with. The dough will be sticky but manageable.

Line 2 baking sheets with parchment paper or lightly butter them.

Preheat the oven to 350° F.

Use a rubber spatula to divide the dough in half. Place each half on a baking sheet. Flour your hands—even the edges with your hands—and pat each batch of dough into a 12 × 5-inch-wide loaf.

Bake the loaves about 15 minutes, or until they are firm to the touch. Take them out of the oven and allow to cool for 10 minutes. Carefully transfer the loaves to a cutting board and cut each one into 18 ½-inch-thick diagonal slices.

Return the slices to the baking sheets, laying them flat on their sides. Bake 5 minutes more, or until lightly toasted.

Transfer the *tozzetti* to a cooling rack to cool completely.

*Variation: For smaller* tozzetti, *divide the dough into quarters and pat the dough into 12 × 2-inch-long loaves. Bake for 8 to 10 minutes, until firm to the touch. Cut the loaves into ½-inch-thick slices.*

# La Domenica

*Brodo di Cappone* (Capon Broth)

*Cappelletti in Brodo* (Little Hats in Broth)

*S*unday morning dawned cloudy and cool in Fabriano, the center for paper making and watermark imprinting for many world currencies. Fabriano is not in Umbria but just over the border, in the region of Le Marche, about an hour's drive from Gubbio. Because of its proximity, the Marchigiani share much in the way of a quiet lifestyle with their Umbrian neighbors.

*Sunday afternoon is a day for friendship and rest.*

*La domenica,* Sunday, is still a day of rest in Italy, a day to be with family, friends, and lovers, a day to dress up in one's finest, to see others and be seen taking the *passeggiata* (a stroll in the piazza or park), and a day to eat well.

Sunday is also a day of worship. From my room in the Janus hotel I could hear the bells of the *campanile* droning out a steady cadence. The power of those bells made me contemplate going to Mass.

The Church of the Misericordia is not far from the hotel, so I walked there, thinking how nice it would be to worship in Italy. On first glance the church disappoints, because it is very modern looking and not what I expected. I like old churches full of precious works of art, brilliant stained-glass windows, soaring majestic pillars, and mosaic-inlaid floors. The Church of the Misericordia is none of that. It is of gray stone post–World War II construction.

Inside it is as stark as a bare tree in winter. A bank of candles was all that illuminated the main altar, and people shuffled back and forth to side altars, their lips trembling with prayers, to light votive candles in hopes of having their most secret requests granted, or in tribute to the souls of their dear departed ones. The wooden pews and kneelers lived up to the name of this church, Misericordia, and would make a far better penance than the standard three Hail Marys; they were hardly the sort of seating one could comfortably doze off in during the sermon.

My fellow worshipers all seemed elderly, and I wondered where the young people were. Clang! Mass began, and I found myself hobbling along, reciting the prayers in Italian as best I could. The priest was elderly, too; he slowly climbed the stairs to the pulpit to deliver a long homily on why the first shall be last and the last first in the kingdom of God. The rest of the ritual was all too familiar to me; I easily maneuvered through the moments of the liturgy. Mass ended with the reminder to go in peace, and I slipped out the back door feeling blessed to be in Fabriano on this overcast Sunday morning.

Walking back to the hotel brought the unmistakable smells of Sunday dinner cooking somewhere nearby. It reminded me of the Sunday dinners at home when all the relatives came to call—not to see me necessarily, but to see Grandma Galasso, who could be found at the stove stirring a rich capon broth bobbing with homemade *cappelletti*. These little homemade pasta "hats" were filled with Grandma's finely ground lemon-flavored meats. They were her trademark, and it just would not have been Sunday without a steaming bowl of *cappelletti in brodo* over which she grated a nice coating of Parmigiano-Reggiano cheese. I knew that somewhere in Fabriano someone was sure to have my favorite dish. I could only imagine what would follow: perhaps a roast pork scented with rosemary, some *fagiolini* (green beans), a nice *insalata mista* (mixed salad), and, since it was Sunday, some kind of sweet *torta di marmellata* (jam tart). *Perfetto!*

Everything in Fabriano is closed on Sunday except for Gelateria Bar del Piano in Piazza Partigrani, which sells *gelato*. In Italy anytime is a good time to have ice cream, but it's especially popular on Sundays when just about everyone walking in the piazza or nearby park is enjoying it in a cone or dish. I walked by the *gelateria* window and couldn't resist. Ice cream is my absolute favorite dessert! Inside, owner Otello Riccioni was more than happy to wait on me. I could see that he was curious about me, too; I guessed that my Italian gave me away as a foreigner. I gave him a snapshot dialogue of my Italian-American heritage, and he told me that he had visited Niagara Falls and Buffalo, New York, and Washington, D.C. When I told him that I grew up in Buffalo, his face lit up because he had friends there. He scooped out samples of eggnog, coffee, and hazelnut *gelato*. Eat fast, he warned, because it melts quickly! He told me that his shop was famous for its creamy *gelato* and I concurred as I gulped down another mouthful and watched a steady parade of happy customers come and go.

Before I left, Otello handed me small jars of amarena cherry jam, ceramic dishes, and candy. Italians are truly generous people. We said good-bye, and I made my way through the park behind the *gelateria* to the hotel with all my little gifts. The park was crammed, just as I knew it would be. Elegantly dressed women sported fine jewelry and colorful scarves; the teen set with spiked hair and the latest jean fashions perched on motorbikes; men in their Sunday suits played cards on benches under the trees or were engaged in a game of *bocce*; and babies were the admiration of all. Everyone was busy doing nothing, which is how it should be on an overcast Sunday—not only in Fabriano but in *tutta l'Italia*.

# Brodo di Cappone

## Capon Broth

Makes 4 quarts

One 5-pound capon,
cut into pieces

1½ teaspoons coarse salt

2 cloves garlic, peeled

1 large onion,
peeled and studded
with 8 whole cloves

1 bay leaf

2 large sprigs each of
parsley and basil,
tied together with
kitchen string

Juice of 1 large lemon

2 large ribs celery with
leaves, cut into
quarters

3 carrots, peeled and cut
into quarters

1 tablespoon
whole black
peppercorns

3 plum tomatoes,
skinned, seeded,
and cut into pieces

Brodo di Cappone *(capon broth) is rich and full-bodied, just the kind of broth needed to complement homemade* cappelletti *(page 77). A capon is a rooster that has been castrated and slaughtered before it is one year old. The meat is very flavorful and has a good deal more white meat than turkey does. Capons can be ordered at your grocery store, or they can be found in the frozen meat section. You can also make the broth with a stewing chicken. (Capon can also be used as the filling for* cappelletti *if you do not wish to use a combination of meats as described in the filling recipe on page 77.) I also serve the cooked capon with a sweet-and-sour (*agrodolce*) sauce, usually based on olive oil and vinegar.*

Place all the ingredients in a large stockpot and cover with cold water. Bring to a boil, lower the heat, and simmer, covered, for 1½ hours, or until the meat is tender. Use a skimmer to skim off any foam that rises to the top and discard it.

With a slotted spoon remove the capon pieces to a bowl. Pour the rest of the soup and ingredients into a cheesecloth-lined strainer over a large bowl. Press on all the solids with the back of a wooden spoon to extract all the juices. Discard the solids.

Cover and refrigerate the broth overnight, then skim off any fat before reheating. The broth can also be frozen for several months.

# Cappelletti in Brodo

## Little Hats in Broth

Makes approximately 150 *cappelletti*; 6 to 8 are plenty for an individual serving

Cappelletti, *or "little hats," are plump meat-filled pasta served in rich capon or chicken broth. The best are said to come from Gubbio where it is a tradition, as in many other parts of Italy, to have them on Christmas. Some historical references claim that the hat shape originated with the pointed hats that Spanish soldiers wore when they invaded Italy in the seventeenth century.* Cappelletti *can be pointed or round; either way, they are a delicate beginning to any Sunday dinner or special occasion. I will not deceive you: These are time-consuming to make, but the reward is in every spoonful. Make them ahead and freeze them. Use large eggs for the dough and lean meats for the filling; do not skimp on the lemon zest. To serve six you will need 2 quarts of the broth (page 76) and three to four dozen of the cappelletti.*

To make the filling: Heat the olive oil over medium-high heat in a sauté pan. Add the meat pieces and brown well on all sides. Do this in batches if necessary; do not crowd the meat, or it will not brown uniformly. As the pieces brown, remove them to a dish.

Grind the meats together in a food processor or meat grinder until they are almost a paste consistency. Transfer the meats to a large bowl and stir in the egg, cheese, parsley, zest, nutmeg, salt, and pepper. Mix well. Cover and refrigerate until ready to fill the pasta rounds.

An alternative for the filling is to use boiled capon (see page 76).

### FILLING

*2 tablespoons
extra-virgin olive oil*

*4 ounces boneless
pork cutlet, cut into
small chunks*

*4 ounces boneless sirloin
steak, cut into small
chunks*

*4 ounces veal roast,
cut into small chunks*

*1 large egg*

*¼ cup grated
Parmigiano-Reggiano
cheese*

*2 tablespoons minced
parsley*

*1 tablespoon grated
lemon zest*

*¼ teaspoon grated
nutmeg*

*Salt to taste*

*Freshly ground black
pepper to taste*

**Cappelletti Dough**

*4 large eggs*

*¼ teaspoon salt*

*3 to 3¼ cups unbleached all-purpose flour*

*Thin slices of lemon*

*Grated Parmigiano-Reggiano cheese for sprinkling*

Grind enough to make ¾ of a pound. Stir in the egg, cheese, parsley, zest, nutmeg, salt, and pepper.

To make the dough: Whirl the eggs and salt together in a food processor or whisk together in a bowl. Gradually add the flour until a ball of dough forms that is not tacky or sticking to your hands. What you want is a smooth dough that is not too dry, or it will be difficult to seal the edges when forming the *cappelletti*.

Knead the dough on a lightly floured work surface until it is a silky and very smooth ball, then let it rest for 30 minutes. Cut the ball into 4 pieces and work with one at time. Flatten each piece with a rolling pin, then run each piece through the rollers of a pasta machine to thin it out. (Alternatively, use a rolling pin to thin the dough.) Do not make it too thin, or the filling will poke through the dough. If you can just see your hand when it is placed behind the sheet of dough, it is thin enough.

I like to use a 1-inch round cutter to cut circles out of the dough; reroll the scraps to make more circles. Place a scant ½ teaspoon of the filling in the center of each circle, then enclose the filling in the dough by forming a half-moon and pinching the edges closed with your fingers. If the dough will not seal, brush a little water or beaten egg white along the edges before sealing. Bring the ends of the half-moon shapes together and seal them.

As you make the *cappelletti*, line them up on towel-lined baking sheets. Do not pile them on top of each other, or they may stick together. Freeze them on the trays and, when frozen, transfer to heavy-duty plastic bags. Take them out as needed and cook in boiling broth just until they bob to the surface. Ladle the *cappelletti* into soup bowls, add a thin slice of lemon, and sprinkle with cheese.

# Lizori's Luscious Lesson

*Insalata di Farro* (Farro Salad)

*Minestra di Farro* (Farro Soup)

*Insalata Calda di Farro e Cece* (Warm Farro and Chickpea Salad)

*Salsa di Funghi e Rosmarino* (Mushroom and Rosemary Sauce)

*Strangozzi* (Big Shoelace Pasta)

*Frascarelli* (Scatters)

*Salsa Arrabbita* (Mad Sauce)

*Creps di Farro* (Farro Crepes)

*Tradition and attention to detail are key to Daniela's cooking.*

e drove through Pissignano Alto on our way to Lizori, a speck of a town that is part of the province. On the way, the town of Trevi came into view, hugging the top of Mount Serano, with its tightly clustered community of buildings spilling down the mountain sides. Trevi is famous for *sedano nero* (black celery) and exceptional olive oil, described in detail on pages 113–115. I imagined that I would be cooking with both today as we neared the storybook town of Lizori, where I was to cook with chef Daniela Bottoni, who owns the most dear little restaurant called Ristorante Camesena that is not far from the therapeutic springs of Campello sul Clitunno, where tourists flock to drink and bathe in its healing waters.

Finally the street came into view, and it was not very wide. It was winding and steep, with contiguous stone buildings lining the way on either side; the van we were in had maybe six inches of room on either side. I just hoped the side-view mirrors would make it! It seemed like an eternity before we got to the restaurant since we inched at a snail's pace to climb higher and higher. Without warning we were rewarded with the most charming view of an endless valley below us, decked out in a carpet of red poppies.

The restaurant terrace had a commanding view of olive trees, manicured farmlands, wheat fields, and even trout farms, and in the distance the view extended all the way to the towns of Montefalco and Assisi!

Daniela greeted us with warmth and enthusiasm. She is a tall woman, with dark olive skin and long jet-black velvet hair. Her black suit accessorized with gold jewelry complemented her hair. She spoke excitedly and rapidly, and I attributed this to a bit of nervousness about cooking for a television audience. I tried to quell those fears, telling her to take her time in explaining the procedure. She was anxious to show me what Umbrians eat, and a table with raw ingredients had been set outside on the terrace near a wood-burning stone oven where bread was being baked. I secretly craved a piece as the smells wafted our way. All of this was making it hard to keep my mind on the task at hand.

Daniela did not even don an apron over her black suit before proceeding to make a rustic-looking Umbrian pasta, *strangozzi*, which means big shoelaces. Her hands tossed all-purpose flour with ground farro flour, an ancient cereal grain similar to spelt that looks like wheat berries and is packed with protein. To the flour she added water but no eggs and no salt, and in a matter of minutes a cushion-soft ball of dough waited to be cut into random-length ribbons. (This is how Daniela makes them, but they can also be made into a thicker rope-shaped pasta). The *strangozzi* was cooked in rapidly boiling salted water until *al dente,* then drained and coated in a sauce made from porcini mushrooms, lard, rosemary, garlic, and salt. Earthy and folksy, this was my kind of cooking.

We moved on to lentils, another hallmark of Umbrian cooking. Lentils arrived in Italy by way of Syria centuries ago and are grown in nearby Castelluccio, famous for its small brown creamy variety. Daniela had cooked the lentils ahead of time and asked me to heat some olive oil in a skillet. We threw in three hefty cloves of garlic, thin slices of the tiniest raw artichokes, and a scoopful of rich chicken stock, and in minutes the dish was ready. At the end we tossed in some delicious-tasting *pomodorini* (cherry tomatoes), salt, and pepper. Each dish was a delicious statement of what Umbrian cooking is all about.

Next, a farro salad was prepared. Like an artist with no prior thought in her head, Daniela created a culinary masterpiece. She spooned the cooked grain on a plate, then topped it with shredded peppery arugula, a drizzle of extra-virgin olive oil, bits of Parmigiano-Reggiano cheese, a whisper of balsamic vinegar, salt, and pepper. Layers of exquisite taste emerged. More farro dishes followed, and I found this little nugget of a grain endearing itself to me as we went along. I sampled farro gnocchi with black truffles and cream sauce, triangular-shaped farro ravioli stuffed with herbs and mushrooms, and for dessert, farro crepes that were as light as a feather and filled with a smooth, slippery pastry cream laced with fresh orange zest and liqueur. Sometimes the crepes are flambéed in Grand Marnier. It was becoming obvious to me that farro plays a huge role in Umbrian cooking; this unassuming-looking grain is responsible for so much that is good, healthy eating in Umbria, and watching Daniela cook was an opportunity to learn about the simple raw ingredients that make up the many culinary layers of Umbrian food and how today's cooks translate their use into the diet. This was unpretentious food at its best, and Daniela prepared and served it all with style and heart.

# Insalata di Farro

## Farro Salad

Serves 4

1 cup farro

¼ cup extra-virgin olive oil plus more to pass at the table

½ teaspoon salt

2 tablespoons balsamic vinegar

8 cherry tomatoes, halved

⅔ cup shredded arugula leaves

Shavings of Parmigiano-Reggiano cheese

*The memory of the farro salad made by Daniela Bottoni in Lizori stayed fresh in my mind even after I returned home. It is a complete meal in terms of a balance of protein with calcium and vegetables. Farro is available in Italian specialty stores, in health food stores, and on the World Wide Web. (See Mail Order Sources, page 199.)*

The fast way to cook farro is to cover it with water the night before you plan to cook it and then the next day drain off the water and put the farro in a 1-quart saucepan. Cover it with fresh water and cook until it is tender but not mushy. This will take about 15 minutes. Drain and transfer to a bowl. Farro can be cooked without presoaking but will need a longer cooking time, about 30 minutes.

Pour the olive oil over the farro and mix it well to coat the grains. Stir in the salt and vinegar. Divide the farro among 4 salad plates. Sprinkle the arugula evenly among the plates. Place 4 tomato halves on each plate and sprinkle with the cheese.

Pass more olive oil at the table to drizzle on top.

# *Minestra di Farro*

## Farro Soup

Serves 4 to 6

*F*arro cooked with a ham bone reminds me of making split pea soup. In Umbria, a prosciutto bone is used to flavor the soup, but any ham bone will do. I can only imagine how good this would be with *sedano nero (black celery)*, but even without it, this is hearty, delicious, and close to Umbrian tradition.

Place the bone, tomatoes, carrots, celery, onion, and parsley in a soup pot. Add enough cold water to cover and bring to a boil. Lower the heat to a simmer, cover the pot, and cook for 1 hour. Remove the ham bone with a slotted spoon and set aside. Strain the broth and vegetables through a colander lined with cheesecloth and set over a bowl. Reserve the carrots and celery.

Return the broth to the soup pot and bring to a boil. Stir in the farro and cook, covered, about 30 minutes, or until the farro is tender but not mushy; it should not disintegrate in the broth.

While the farro is cooking, remove the meat from the bone and cut it into pieces. Cut the carrots and celery into small pieces. Add the ham, carrots, and celery to the soup pot once the farro is cooked. Season the soup with salt and pepper, and serve hot. Pass the cheese and olive oil for sprinkling and drizzling on top of the soup.

*1 meaty ham or
  prosciutto bone*

*4 plum tomatoes,
  coarsely chopped*

*2 carrots, peeled and
  cut into quarters*

*2 ribs celery with leaves,
  cut into quarters*

*1 medium onion, peeled*

*1 small bunch Italian
  parsley*

*1 cup farro*

*Salt to taste*

*Freshly ground pepper
  to taste*

*Grated pecorino cheese*

*Extra-virgin olive oil*

# Insalata Calda di Farro e Cece

## Warm Farro and Chickpea Salad

Serves 6

½ cup farro

⅔ cup dried chickpeas

3 garlic cloves, peeled

4 or 5 sprigs Italian parsley, stemmed, plus extra for garnish

3 fresh sage leaves

2 sprigs fresh rosemary, needles only

¼ cup extra-virgin olive oil plus extra for drizzling

¼ teaspoon dried oregano

4 ounces cremini or button mushrooms, thinly sliced

8 cherry tomatoes, halved

¼ cup reserved cooking water from the chickpeas

¼ teaspoon fine sea salt

*Here is more evidence that farro is enjoying a comeback in today's kitchens. The inspiration for this warm farro and chickpea salad comes from another Umbrian chef, Donatella Lauteri. Begin the process the day before by soaking the farro and the chickpeas.*

Place the farro in a bowl and cover with water. In another bowl, cover the chickpeas with water. Allow both to soak overnight. Doing this will eliminate a long cooking time.

The next day, drain the water from the chickpeas and transfer them to a pot. Cover with clean water and cook for 15 minutes, or just until they are tender and the outer skin slips off easily. Drain, reserving ¼ cup of the cooking liquid, and set aside. Repeat the process for the farro, cooking it about 15 minutes or just until *al dente*. Depending on the farro, it may cook in even less time. It should have a bit of a bite and not be mushy.

Mince the garlic, parsley, sage, and rosemary together.

Preheat the oven to 350° F.

Heat the olive oil in a sauté pan. Stir in the minced herb mixture and oregano. Cook for 2 minutes, stirring occasionally. Stir in the mushrooms and cook until they soften and begin to give off their liquid. Stir in the tomatoes and cook 2 minutes more. Stir in the chickpeas, farro, and reserved chickpea cooking water. Stir and cook 3 minutes more. Stir in the salt, pepper, and red pepper flakes, and cook 1 minute longer. Keep the mixture warm while toasting the bread.

Place the bread slices on a baking sheet and toast for 5 to 7 minutes, until golden brown.

Place 2 slices of toasted bread side by side on each of 6 salad plates. Evenly divide and spoon the farro mixture over the bread slices. Garnish with extra parsley and drizzle a little olive oil over the top.

Serve immediately.

*Freshly ground black pepper to taste*

*¼ teaspoon dried red pepper flakes*

*12 small slices baguette-style bread, cut ½ inch thick*

# Salsa di Funghi e Rosmarino

## Mushroom and Rosemary Sauce

Makes 3½ cups

*½ cup extra-virgin olive oil plus more to pass at the table*

*2 large cloves garlic, minced*

*4 tablespoons rosemary needles, minced*

*1 pound fresh porcini or portobello mushrooms, stemmed, wiped clean, and cut into ½-inch-thick slices*

*1¼ cups beef broth*

*Fine sea salt to taste*

*Freshly ground black pepper to taste*

*Strangozzi (see recipe on page 89)*

*This perfumy porcini mushroom and rosemary sauce, made by Daniela Bottoni to top homemade* strangozzi, *is quick to put together. Fresh porcini mushrooms are not difficult to find, but they are expensive. As an alternative you can use fresh portobello, which are readily available, but the taste will not be exactly the same. The sauce is enough for 1 pound of the* strangozzi *(page 89) or* pappardelle *(page 62).*

Heat the olive oil in a large sauté pan. When it begins to shimmer, stir in the garlic and rosemary. Swirl the mixture with a wooden spoon over medium heat for a few minutes to release the rosemary flavor. Your kitchen will smell like the forest.

Stir in the mushrooms. Do not be alarmed when the oil disappears; mushrooms are notorious for soaking up oil. Continue to cook over medium heat until the mushrooms begin to soften and give off some of their liquid. Stir in the broth, salt, and pepper. Lower the heat to a simmer and cook the sauce for 3 or 4 minutes, just until everything is hot.

Keep the sauce hot while the *strangozzi* are cooking. Toss the *strangozzi* with the sauce and serve. Pass the olive oil for drizzling on top.

*N*ote: *Pasta made with farro flour absorbs a lot of sauce.*

# *Strangozzi*

## Big Shoelace Pasta

Makes 1¾ pounds; serves 6

Strangozzi *means big shoelaces. The story goes that the name* strangozzi *is derived from unhappy taxpayers who, when they saw the tax man coming, wanted to take a rope or shoelace to strangle him! It is a typical Umbrian pasta made with a combination of unbleached all-purpose flour, farro flour, and water. This produces an oatmeal-colored dough with visible flecks of farro flour. If you do not have farro flour (see Mail Order Sources, page 199), use unbleached all-purpose flour for the recipe.*

*The dough is easily made in a food processor or on a board using the "fontana" method of creating a hole in the center of the flour, pouring in the water, and drawing the flour in from the sides until a ball of dough is formed. The dough is rolled and cut like fettuccine; the recipe was tested on a manual pasta machine using the fettuccine cutter. Some cooks like to pinch off small pieces of the dough and roll them into round ropes of various lengths, resembling shoelaces. Done this way, the ropes will be thicker than passing the dough through the rollers of the pasta machine. No salt is added to the dough; it is added to the water just before cooking the* strangozzi. *Toss it with the mushroom and rosemary sauce on page 88.*

*3 cups unbleached all-purpose flour*

*1 cup farro flour*

*1¼ cups water, or more if necessary*

Mix the flours together on a board or whirl them together in a food processor. To make the dough by hand using the *fontana* method, make a hole with your hand in the middle of the flour. Pour the water into the center and begin bringing the flour into the center with your hands to create a ball of dough. Add more water if necessary to make a smooth ball that is not sticky. Knead the dough on the board with your hands for several minutes. Cover it and let it rest for 30 minutes before proceeding with the rolling and cutting.

If you make the dough in a food processor, add the water slowly through the feed tube until a ball forms and leaves the sides of the bowl. Remove the dough to a work surface, knead it a few times with your hands, and let it rest, covered, for 30 minutes.

Divide the dough into 4 pieces and work with 1 piece at a time; keep the rest covered so it does not dry out.

Use a rolling pin to flatten the dough pieces, then pass each piece through the flat rollers of a pasta machine. Follow the directions for your specific machine to achieve a thin sheet of dough; it is number 7 on most machines. Cut the sheet in half crosswise and hang the sheets over dowel rods positioned between two chairs to dry slightly. If the pasta sheets are too wet, they will not cut cleanly when put through the cutters. I allow the sheets to dry as long as it takes me to finish rolling out the last piece of dough, about 10 minutes.

When the sheets are still damp, pass them through the fettuccine cutter and hang the strands on the dowel rods. Be sure to separate the strands from one another. If you want to store the *strangozzi* for later use, let them dry thoroughly on the rods; they are dry enough when the ends begin to curl up. Insufficient drying will cause the pasta to get moldy!

To remove the *strangozzi* from the dowel rods, carefully lift up each rod, tilting it and sliding the strands with your hands onto a large sheet of aluminum foil. Close the foil, crimping it loosely, and store in a cool, dry place. It will keep for several months.

If cooking the *strangozzi* immediately, spread the strands out on lightly floured kitchen towels.

To cook, bring 4 to 6 quarts of water to a boil in a pasta pot or other large pot. Add 1 tablespoon of salt per pound of pasta, so if

*Penne Tartufate* (Penne with Truffles and Cream), made with spaghetti, page 8

*Insalata di Farro* (Farro Salad), page 84

*Torta di Cioccolata all'Olio d'Oliva* (Chocolate Olive Oil Cake), pages 118–19

*Frittatina di Verdure* (Vegetable Frittata), pages 125–26

*Braciolette di Maiale alla Spoletina* (Pork Chops Spoleto Style), page 131

*Tegamaccio* (Lago Trasimeno Fish Stew), page 165

*Brustengo* (Gubbian Flat Bread), page 151

*Pere al Sagrantino* (Pears Poached in Sagrantino Wine), page 185

you are cooking all the pasta this recipe makes, you will need to add 1¾ tablespoons of salt.

Add the *strangozzi* to the boiling water, stir once, and cook for 3 or 4 minutes. Remember that fresh pasta cooks very quickly. The *strangozzi* are done when they are cooked through but are not mushy.

Drain in a colander and toss with the mushroom and rosemary sauce on page 88 or use a sauce of your choice.

# Frascarelli

## Scatters

Serves 4 to 6

**2½–3 cups
unbleached flour**

**¼ teaspoon fine sea salt,
plus 1 tablespoon**

**4 large eggs,
slightly beaten**

Frascarelli, *or scatters, remind me of pastina, that tiny dot of a pasta used in soup. Traditionally* frascarelli *were made from the scraps of dough scraped up from the pasta board after making* strangozzi *(page 89). Serve with homemade tomato sauce or spicy* arrabbiata sauce, *opposite.*

Mix the flour with the salt then spread it in a thin layer on a large work surface. Use your hands to sprinkle the beaten eggs over the flour. Then use your hands to move the flour over the egg to create tiny beads of pasta. Place them in the sieve or strainer and shake to remove excess flour. What you are left with are the frascarelli—tiny, odd-shaped beads of pasta. Place them on a towel-lined baking sheet as you remove them from the sieve.

Bring 4 quarts of water to a boil. Stir in 1 tablespoon of the salt. Cook the frascarelli for 1 or 2 minutes. Drain well and serve tossed with tomato sauce.

# Salsa Arrabbiata

## Mad Sauce

Makes 3 cups

Salsa arrabbiata *gets its name from the use of hot red pepper flakes in the sauce. It is perfect for* frascarelli, *opposite.*

Preheat the oven to 400° F.

Cut the tomatoes in half. Place them cut side down on a baking sheet and bake for 10 to 15 minutes or until they soften slightly. Transfer the tomatoes to a food processor and pulse until very smooth.

In a medium saucepan, heat the olive oil. Add the garlic and red pepper flakes and cook until the garlic is soft. Add the tomatoes and cook for 10 minutes over low heat. Set a sieve over a bowl and strain the sauce, pressing with a wooden spoon to extract as much liquid as possible. Discard the solids left behind.

Add the salt, pepper, and basil. Stir to blend well. The sauce is best when freshly made but can be refrigerated for up to a week.

*N*ote: *This sauce is also good over any short cut of chunky pasta.*

3 pounds fresh plum tomatoes

3 tablespoons extra-virgin olive oil

3 large cloves garlic, minced

1¼ teaspoons hot red pepper flakes

1 teaspoon fine sea salt

¼ teaspoon coarse black pepper

⅓ cup minced basil leaves

# *Creps di Farro*

## Farro Crêpes

Serves 4 to 5

CRÊPE BATTER

¾ *cup farro flour*

*3 large eggs*

*1 cup whole milk*

*Unsalted butter
for frying*

PASTRY CREAM

¼ *cup sugar*

*4 egg yolks*

*2 tablespoons
unbleached
all-purpose flour*

*1 cup whole milk*

*Grated zest of
1 large orange*

*1 tablespoon orange
liqueur or vanilla
extract*

*1 teaspoon unsalted
butter*

GARNISH

½ *cup honey*

¼ *cup slivered almonds*

*These dessert crêpes made with farro flour were the crowning glory of the day spent cooking with Daniela Bottoni at Ristorante Camesena. They are at once elegant and rustic, with a light, not-too-sweet orange-flavored pastry cream that is easy to make. Farro flour is available in specialty stores and by mail order (see page 199). As a last resort use unbleached all-purpose flour.*

To make the batter: Mix the flour and eggs together with a whisk in a medium-size bowl. I use one with a spout so I can pour the batter directly into the pan. Whisk in the milk until a smooth batter is obtained.

Melt 1 teaspoon of butter in a 7-inch nonstick skillet over medium heat. Pour a scant ¼ cup of the batter into the pan and swirl the pan to make sure the bottom is evenly coated with the batter and there are no holes. Allow the crêpe to cook until the edges begin to brown slightly and the top of the crêpe is firm to the touch. Slide it out onto a piece of waxed paper. Continue making crêpes, using a little butter in the pan each time if needed to prevent sticking. As you make them, stack the crêpes between sheets of waxed paper. You should be able to get 10 crêpes from the batter. Set them aside or cover with aluminum foil and refrigerate for up to 3 days before serving. Be sure to allow them to come to room temperature.

To make the pastry cream: Whisk the sugar, egg yolks, and flour together in the top of a double boiler off the heat. Make sure the mixture is smooth and there are no lumps. Slowly whisk in the milk.

Fill the bottom of the double boiler with water. Place the pan over the base of the double boiler, making sure the water in the base does not touch the bottom of the top pan or you may run the risk of curdling the eggs. Stir the mixture over medium heat until it begins to thicken; this may take about 5 minutes. The pastry cream should be thick enough to coat a spoon.

Pour the pastry cream into a bowl and stir in the orange zest, liqueur, and butter. Place a small piece of waxed paper over the top of the bowl to prevent a skin from forming on the pastry cream. At this point the pastry cream can be refrigerated for up to 4 days before using.

To assemble the crêpes: Lay each crêpe out flat on a cutting board. Spread about 2 tablespoons of the pastry cream on each crêpe, fold it in half to make a half-moon, and then fold once more to create a fan shape. Place the crêpes on individual dessert plates. Serve 2 per person.

Warm the honey over low heat in a small saucepan. Use a spoon to drizzle it over the crêpes. Sprinkle on the almonds and serve immediately.

*Variations: For a simpler presentation dust the top of the crêpes with confectioners' sugar and garnish with a strawberry.*

*I have substituted eggnog for milk in the pastry cream, with delicious results.*

# Perugia the Proud

*Strufoli* (Honey Balls)

*Serpentone delle Monache Cappuccine* (The Capuchin Nuns'
   Serpent)

*Torcolo di San Costanzo* (San Costanzo Fruit-Filled Sweet Bread)

*Torta di Frutta Fresca* (Fresh Fruit Tart)

*P*erugia, the energetic capital of the region of Umbria, is perched on a hilltop 1500 feet above sea level and has a commanding view of the pristine Umbrian plain. It is a fascinating city with a turbulent history, one prone to lots of warring factions from the Etruscans to the Romans (who encased the town with walls built of massive stone to protect it from enemy invaders) to the wrath of Pope Paul III, who destroyed the homes of the ruling Baglioni family and built the formidable Rocca Paolino (Rock of Paul) on their ruins as a reminder to the stubborn Perugini that the Church would not tolerate their existence as a free commune instead of a papal state. As if that were not enough, in the sixteenth century the Perugini were slapped with a tax on salt in the so-called Salt War, which they defiantly refused to pay. Not to be defeated, they eliminated the use of salt in their bread—and to this day it is made without salt.

I feel very comfortable in Perugia, having visited it often. I feel welcome and at home here. Like the Perugini who work here every day or study at the university, my favorite route takes me along the main street and lifeline of Perugia, the Corso Vannucci, named for the city's famous painter Pietro Vannucci, also called Perugino. Along this street a blend of fascinating cityscapes commands attention: Look to the left or right and there are steep, twisted, and dark medieval streets branching off that beg for prolonged exploration. On the *corso* itself there are beautifully carved Renaissance doors that open into palatial palaces. At the end of the corso is the pride and symbol of the city, the magnificent Fontana Maggiore, a thirteenth-century fountain crafted by Nicola and his son Giovanni

Pisano. The base of the fountain tells the story of the seasons with its depictions of sowing crops, tilling the soil, hunting scenes, and the grape harvest. The upper section depicts medieval life as told through biblical and historic figures. Across from the fountain is the austere Palazzo dei Priori, Perugia's civic palace whose main doorway is guarded by twin griffins *(il grifo)*, another symbol of the city.

The area around the fountain, the Piazza Quattro Novembre, is always abuzz with activity; there are students on their way to classes at the University for Foreigners, shoppers, and tourists who sit on the steps of Perugia's various historic buildings to eat their lunch, jot their impressions of the city on postcards, or just people-watch. It is my favorite area, too. I like to walk beyond the Piazza Quattro Novembre, past the unfinished facade of the Church of San Lorenzo, and up the hill to a wonderful belvedere where a panorama of neat patchwork quilt-like farms and olive groves dot the still landscape below. In the distance, Assisi, the spiritual home of Saint Francis, can be seen.

Besides all this historic importance, sweet cravings draw me to Perugia and, in particular, to Sandri's, one of the most elegant and famous pastry shops and bars in Italy, and the oldest one in Umbria. The Perugini are just as proud of their edible art as they are of their historic monuments. They frequent Sandri's in droves, sitting outside at shady tables, indulging in heavenly confections while watching the world go by, or standing at its ornate bar sipping espresso. I like to sit in its cozy, dark-wood-paneled interior with its beautiful vaulted, frescoed ceilings, and drool at the array of *dolci*. Everything for a sweet tooth is here, from biscotti to *cornetti* to tiramisù, along with huge glass wall cases of chocolates and jellied candies. Need a Sacher torte to take home or give to a friend? It will be wrapped beautifully in brilliant red paper and tied with a gold bow. The glistening fresh fruit tarts are my favorite; they are a frequent window display and are part of the story of Sandri's culinary history. Each season the window displays change; sometimes there are tiers of dome-shaped cheese breads or cheesecakes with glistening ruby red strawberries on top, or there are dense chocolate cakes filled with ganache and sporting huge bows made out of chocolate.

I have a history with this place, too. It was here that I first learned how to make the eels of Lago Trasimeno *(anguille)* out of almond paste in the *laboratorio* with my teacher, pastry chef Carla Schucani. Signora Carla is all business in the kitchen; she directs like a general and turns out magnificent creations for Sandri's display windows. It is no wonder that she is such a whiz; it was her family who established Sandri's and taught her the delicate art of pastry-making from a young age. Her large mannish hands shape tricky pastry dough so swiftly that your full concentration is needed to keep up with her. Signora Carla's complete dedication and pride in her art shines through.

Even more amazing is Signora Carla's use of the windows to commemorate special events, such as the annual Umbria Jazz Festival which is interpreted with her creation of drums, piano, and trumpets made entirely from sugar and egg whites. Or her creation of some of the city's most famous landmarks, such as the Fontana Maggiore—constructed out of white, dark, and milk chocolate! These windows make a powerful and complete statement about the authenticity of Sandri's confections, and they transfix and lure the passerby: Suddenly, in the middle of the morning, one is hungry, and the effect is complete.

When visiting Perugia, with all its charm and civility, it is hard to imagine the many battles and vendettas waged here in the name of power; but given its history, it is easy to see why the Perugini are fiercely competitive and protective of a city that has defined their character and given them much to be proud of.

# *Strufoli*

## Honey Balls

Serves 8 to 10

1¼ cups unbleached
all-purpose flour

1½ teaspoons baking
powder

¼ cup sugar

¼ teaspoon fine sea salt

5 tablespoons
extra-virgin olive oil

2 large eggs,
lightly beaten

1 tablespoon
grated lemon zest

2 cups honey

Vegetable oil for frying

½ cup slivered almonds

¼ teaspoon
ground cinnamon

Candied sprinkles

*This version of* strufoli *from Perugia is similar to others found in pastry shops all over Italy. Small rounds of fried dough, coated in honey, are shaped into a ring and decorated with almonds and candy sprinkles. They are a holiday treat, and tiers of them make a colorful display in Sandri's windows.*

Make the dough in a bowl or food processor by combining the flour, baking powder, sugar, and salt. Add the olive oil, eggs, and zest by hand or whirl in the processor until a ball of soft dough forms.

Gather up the dough, which will feel tacky, and cover it with plastic wrap. Refrigerate for 1 hour to make it easier to work with.

Divide the dough into 4 pieces and keep the rest covered. Roll each piece under the palm of your hand into a long rope the width of your middle finger. Cut the rope with a knife into small pieces about the size of a marble. Set aside.

Heat the honey in a heavy pot and keep warm.

Heat the vegetable oil to 375° F in a deep fryer or heavy-duty pot. Drop a small piece of the dough into the oil to test the temperature. If the dough rises immediately and browns quickly, the oil is ready.

Fry the balls in the oil a handful at a time, until golden brown. Remove the balls with a slotted spoon or the drain basket and place on absorbent paper.

Quickly toss the balls into the honey and turn to coat them well. With a slotted spoon transfer the balls to a serving dish. While continuing to fry and coat the balls, fashion them with wet hands when cool enough to handle into a large ring on the serving plate. Wetting your hands will give you more control.

Sprinkle the almonds and cinnamon over the ring and scatter the candied sprinkles. To eat, break off pieces with your hands or use a knife.

# Serpentone delle Monache Cappuccine

## The Capuchin Nuns' Serpent

Makes 1 large snake

### DOUGH

1 cup warm water (110° F)

1½ teaspoons active dry yeast

2 tablespoons extra-virgin olive oil

¼ teaspoon salt

2 tablespoons sugar

3 cups unbleached all-purpose flour

### FILLING

⅓ cup golden raisins

⅓ cup dark raisins

3 tablespoons vin santo or brandy

½ cup coarsely chopped walnuts

5 dried figs, stemmed and diced

5 prunes, diced

Serpentone *(the serpent) is a sign of fertility and also a sign of a good and abundant harvest, and it is also another confectionery specialty of Perugia. Sweet-filled serpent-shaped breads were originally made by Capuchin nuns, who sold them to the public in order to get needed funds for their monastery. The dough is made quickly in a food processor or by hand. Other versions are made with egg whites, sugar, and ground almonds, and are called* anguille di Lago Trasimeno, *the eels of Lake Trasimeno.*

Line a baking sheet with a piece of parchment paper and set aside. To make the dough: Pour the water into the bowl of a food processor fitted with the steel blade or pour the water into a large bowl. Sprinkle the yeast over the water and pulse or stir to dissolve it. Add the olive oil, salt, and sugar, and blend well. Pulse or stir in the flour, 1 cup at a time. Knead the dough for about 5 minutes or until smooth. Three cups of flour should give you a nonsticky smooth dough. If the dough is too tacky, add a bit more flour, 1 tablespoon at a time, until the dough is smooth and nonsticky.

Transfer the dough to a bowl and cover tightly with plastic wrap. Let the dough rise in a warm (75° F) but not too hot area until doubled in size.

Meanwhile, make the filling: In a small bowl, combine the raisins and *vin santo,* and allow to soak for 30 minutes. In another bowl, combine the walnuts, figs, prunes, apples, olive oil, and sugar. Add the raisins and all the liquid, and combine well. Set aside.

Punch down the dough and transfer it to a work surface. Roll out the dough into an 18-inch circle and spread the filling ingredients evenly over the surface to within 2 inches of the edges. Roll the dough up on itself into a tight jelly roll, tucking in the sides as you roll. Lift the roll and place it on the baking sheet. With your hands create an **s** shape with the dough, but leave the head area larger than the tail area.

Insert the coffee beans or candied cherries into the head area to form the eyes. Use the almond for the tongue. Cover the *serpentone* with a towel and allow it to rise about 45 minutes.

Preheat the oven to 375° F.

Brush the *serpentone* with the egg wash and sprinkle the sugar evenly over the dough.

Bake for 30 to 35 minutes on the middle rack of your oven. If the top browns too much while baking, cover the dough loosely with a piece of aluminum foil. The *serpentone* is done when a cake tester inserted in the center comes out clean.

Transfer the *serpentone* to a wire rack to cool slightly. This is best served warm.

*2 Golden Delicious apples, peeled and thinly sliced*

*1 tablespoon extra-virgin olive oil*

*2 tablespoons sugar*

DECORATION

*2 coffee beans or candied cherries*

*1 whole almond*

*1 egg and 1 tablespoon water, lightly beaten*

*Coarse white sugar*

# Torcolo di San Costanzo

## San Costanzo Fruit-Filled Sweet Bread

Makes 1 large ring-shaped sweet bread

¼ *cup raisins*

1 *cup warm milk (110° F)*

1 *tablespoon active dry yeast*

8 *tablespoons (1 stick) unsalted butter, melted and cooled*

¾ *cup sugar*

3 *large eggs, lightly beaten, plus 1 yolk*

½ *teaspoon salt*

½ *cup finely diced citron*

1 *tablespoon aniseed*

¼ *cup pine nuts*

*Grated zest of 2 large lemons*

6 *cups (approximately) unbleached all-purpose flour*

Torcolo *is the classic sweet bread of Perugia, made on January 29 to commemorate the feast of its patron, San Costanzo. It is also traditional for a man to give this bread to his lover. The story goes that if the statue of San Costanzo winks at you on the day the bread is presented, the couple will marry within the year. It's nice to speculate that this is true and that the bread's ring shape is symbolic of the wedding ring, but even if this is not the case, it is easily made for any occasion in a stand mixer. The dough is very heavy and laden with citron, raisins, and aniseed. The dough can also be made by hand in a bowl. Start the process early in the day.*

Butter a 9 × 2-inch ring mold and set aside.

Place the raisins in a small bowl, cover with water, and let soak for 30 minutes to plump them. Drain off the water, mince the raisins, and set aside.

Pour the milk into the bowl of a heavy-duty stand mixer fitted with the paddle attachment. Sprinkle the yeast over the milk and quickly whisk it to dissolve the yeast. On low speed, blend in the butter, sugar, whole eggs, salt, citron, raisins, aniseed, pine nuts, and zest. Begin adding the flour, 1 cup at a time, on low speed. Blend well before adding the next cup. Continue adding flour until the dough forms around the paddle and leaves the sides of the bowl. Do not add so much flour that the dough becomes tough and too dry. It should not be sticky on your hands but just feel slightly tacky.

Remove the dough from the bowl and knead it with your hands on a slightly floured surface several times and form it into a ball. Place the dough in a large buttered bowl and cover it tightly with plastic wrap. Allow the dough to rise in a not-too-hot area (75° F is ideal) until it is double in size; this could take 2 to 3 hours.

Preheat the oven to 375° F.

Punch down the dough with your fists. Transfer it to a work surface and roll it into a 23- or 24-inch-long rope. Bring the 2 ends together and pinch them closed. Place the dough in the prepared ring mold. Cover with a clean towel and let rise for 30 minutes. If you do not have a ring mold, place the dough on a greased baking sheet and place a well-greased 2½- to 3-inch round ovenproof dish in the center of the dough to keep its shape while baking.

When ready to bake, beat the remaining egg yolk with a fork and use a pastry brush to paint the top of the bread. This will give the finished bread a nice shiny look.

Bake the bread for 30 to 40 minutes, or until the bread is firm to the touch and sounds hollow when tapped. You can also insert a cake tester in the center of the bread, and if it comes out clean, the bread is done. If the top browns too fast while baking, cover it loosely with a piece of aluminum foil.

Allow the bread to cool in the pan for 20 minutes. Use a butter knife to loosen the sides of the bread from the mold. Invert the mold and remove the bread to a cooling rack. Allow the bread to cool completely.

If baking the bread on a baking sheet, carefully remove the greased bowl in the center before transferring the bread to the cooling rack.

# Torta di Frutta Fresca

## Fresh Fruit Tart

Serves 8 to 10

CREMA PASTICCERIA
(PASTRY CREAM)

*1⅔ cups whole milk*

*Grated zest of 1 large
lemon*

*6 egg yolks plus
1 whole egg*

*¾ cup sugar*

*¼ cup plus
1 tablespoon
unbleached all-
purpose flour*

*¼ teaspoon salt*

*1 tablespoon
unsalted butter*

*One ½-inch piece of
vanilla bean or
2 teaspoons vanilla or
almond extract*

PASTA FROLLA
(PASTRY DOUGH)

*2 cups unbleached
all-purpose flour*

*½ cup sugar*

*¼ teaspoon salt*

*M*aking a fruit tart like those in Sandri's display windows is not difficult. We begin by making a short-cut pastry dough that is fitted into a tart shell pan and then baked. A velvety pastry cream is spread over the tart, and, finally, a variety of fresh seasonal fruits are arranged on top. Both the dough and the pastry cream can be made ahead of time. Be artistic in how you arrange the fruit, mixing and matching blackberries, cherries, raspberries, plums, nectarines, and peaches to achieve vivid color. Signora Carla would be proud!

To make the pastry cream: Pour the milk into a 1-quart saucepan and stir in the lemon zest. Heat over low heat just until bubbles start to appear at the edge of the pan. Remove the pan from the heat and set it aside. Beat the egg yolks, egg, and sugar in a bowl with a handheld mixer until the eggs look very pale yellow. Slowly beat in the flour and salt until well blended. Pour the heated milk into the bowl and stir with a wooden spoon to mix the ingredients well. Return the mixture to the saucepan and cook over medium heat, stirring constantly until the mixture coats the back of a spoon. Remove the saucepan from the heat and stir in the butter. Add the vanilla bean or stir in the vanilla. Pour the pastry cream into a clean bowl and cover with a piece of waxed paper or plastic wrap to prevent a skin from forming. Refrigerate until needed. This can be made at least 3 days ahead of time. Remove the vanilla bean before using the pastry cream.

To make the dough: Pulse the flour, sugar, salt, and butter together in the bowl of a food processor fitted with the dough blade or blend the ingredients together in a large bowl with a fork or pastry blender until the butter is in small bits. The whole idea here is to coat the flour proteins with the butter to prevent gluten from forming, which would make a tough pastry dough, so be sure the butter is very cold.

Beat the egg yolk and vinegar together with a fork in a small bowl. Add to the food processor with the motor running (or to the bowl if you are making this by hand) and process or blend until a rough-looking dough starts to form. Slowly add enough cold water for a ball of dough to form that holds together. It does not need to be a complete ball, but it should not crumble when you gather it up.

Cover the dough with plastic wrap and refrigerate for at least 1 hour or overnight to make it easier to roll.

Preheat the oven to 400° F.

Lightly butter a 10-inch tart pan with a removable bottom and set aside.

Flatten the dough with a rolling pin and roll it between 2 sheets of waxed paper into a 12-inch circle. Dust the top of the dough lightly with flour, then fold it in fourths. Lift the dough and position it with the point of the fold in the center of the tart shell. Unfold the dough and fit it into the pan, allowing the excess to drape over the sides. Trim the edges even with a scissors and press the dough evenly at the top of the pan. Poke holes in the tart shell with a fork to allow air to escape during baking. Place a sheet of foil over the top of the dough and weigh it down with dried beans or rice; this will help prevent the tart shell from puffing up as it bakes.

Bake the tart shell for 10 minutes, then remove the foil and beans and bake 3 minutes more, or until light golden brown. Let the tart shell cool to room temperature on a cooling rack.

Heat the apricot jam until it melts. Cool slightly, then brush the jam over the base of the shell; this will seal it and prevent it from becoming soggy when the pastry cream is added.

*5 tablespoons cold unsalted butter, cut into bits*

*1 large egg yolk*

*1 tablespoon white vinegar*

*3 tablespoons cold water*

*2 tablespoons apricot jam*

*Assorted fresh fruits (blackberries, cherries, raspberries, plums, nectarines, peaches), cut into thin slices or left whole to arrange on top of the tart*

*Confectioners' sugar for sprinkling*

Spread the pastry cream in the shell. Chill, uncovered, for 2 hours.

Arrange the selection of fruits on top of the pastry cream in a decorative pattern. Sometimes I also add long ribbons of shaved chocolate on top of the fruit, but this is optional. Sprinkle the tart with confectioners' sugar. To serve, cut it into wedges.

# Ode to Olive Oil

*Marinata d'Olio d'Oliva Extra-Virgine* (Extra-Virgin Olive Oil Marinade)

*Pinzimonio* (Raw Vegetables with Extra-Virgin Olive Oil)

*Torta di Cioccolata all'Olio d'Oliva* (Chocolate Olive-Oil Cake)

*Oil and water do not mix; just ask Fabio.*

*H*is Holiness would like the olive oil sent to the Vatican." So goes the traditional papal request for extra-virgin olive oil from Umbria. For centuries, even popes recognized and appreciated the superiority of the olive oil from trees in this region, and paid farmers to plant them on the middle hills and in the chalky soil of the Umbrian countryside. To this day Umbrian olive oil graces the table in the Vatican and is considered some of the best in Italy. But even before popes recognized its worth, it was held in high regard, and its branches became a symbol of peace for the world. The ancient Etruscans, Greeks, and Romans understood olive oil's worthiness for culinary purposes, but its use also extended to oil for their lamps, for rubbing on the body, and as a profitable trading product.

Yet in the American kitchen the role of olive oil is misunderstood; confusion reigns as to whether to cook with extra-virgin, virgin, or pomace. Should one cook with extra-virgin olive oil or reserve it solely for dressing salads? Can it be used to deep-fry foods? Which is the best one to buy? Where should it be stored?

I have been cooking with low-acidity extra-virgin olive oil for years, and I know what I like—fruity olive oil for salads and peppery olive oil for sautéing. Selecting olive oil is a lot like selecting a bottle of wine. It can be a daunting task, but if you know what you like, the job becomes easier. And just as there are hundreds of wines to choose from, so, too, many choices exist for olive oil.

Everything is dependent on your palate and whether or not you like fruity, dense, spicy, mild, or peppery as a flavor characteristic. The best way to determine this is to sample different types of olive oil from various regions of Italy. Generally speaking, the farther south one travels in Italy, the fruitier, denser, and greener the oil will be, and as one travels north, the oil is lighter in color, less dense, and milder. By definition—and by Italian law—extra-virgin olive oil must not contain more that 1 percent acidity, must come from the first pressing of the olives, and must be extracted without heat. Other grades have higher amounts of acidity and may come from multiple pressings. In the case of pomace, which is the pulp that remains after pressing the olives, any remaining oil is extracted with the use of solvents. This oil is refined and blended with a small percentage of virgin olive oil (higher acidity) and sold at much cheaper prices, but in my estimation you get what you pay for.

Someone who knows a lot about the production of Umbrian olive oil is Fabio Ciri, and I was anxious for him to give me a tasting lesson in his olive oil mill, Mulino della Torre, which is not far from Spoleto. Fabio's family has been producing extra-virgin olive oil and grinding grain into flour for many years. The mill for grinding corn into flour is still in operation and uses only water power. The mill originally used for the production of olive oil is now an olive oil museum. This is where I took part in the tasting.

Fabio is the perfect teacher: His demeanor is one of gentleness and he is soft-spoken and mild-mannered. His piercing eyes tell you how proud he is to educate all who come to learn about olive oil. The museum is full of old equipment, from Herculean-looking grinding stones weighing about a ton, to the simple *rete da raccolta* (nets) placed around the base of the trees to catch the olives that fall down. Hanging on the wall of the museum are the old green-and-white-striped sacks that the *olivara* (olive picker) wore to catch the olives and the *pettine*, or combs, used to rake them from their branches. There is also a sanctuary of old *zici*, the large terra-cotta containers used to hold the oil.

We were ready for the tasting. Fabio set a table with a variety of extra-virgin olive oils and poured samples into small glasses. I saw pieces of Granny Smith apples sitting on a plate and asked what they were for. They were to clean the palate between each tasting. First, we warmed the olive oil by holding the glass in our cupped hands; next we looked at the color by holding the glass to the light. Umbrian extra-virgin olive oil has a greenish hue. The smell was next. Fruity, fresh, and flowery are some of the terms used to describe the various scents we inhaled. The next part was a well-orchestrated event: To really taste olive oil correctly, you must take a sip and roll it around in your mouth—but don't swallow yet! Taste it at the tip of your tongue, the root of your mouth, the center of the tongue, and the back of the tongue. Now swallow for a throat "finish." The different areas of the mouth produce a variety of taste sensations. Fabio used words like nutty, peppery, heavy, intense, light, sweet, earthy, grassy, and buttery. If you follow this technique, you will come to appreciate the many properties of olive oil.

A trip to Umbria is not necessary to buy olive oil; it is available in the United States as are olive oils from other regions of Italy. Find them in Italian grocery stores, by mail order (see page 199) and on the Internet. Then conduct your own olive oil tasting.

A word about storing olive oil: It is best to keep it in a cool, dark place, not in the refrigerator where temperature extremes can affect its flavor. Olive oil is best used within a year of its purchase, or else it can become rancid, so it's best to buy only a small supply. Follow these guidelines, and you will be using and enjoying olive oil according to Italian tradition.

# Marinata d'Olio d'Oliva Extra-Virgine

## Extra-Virgin Olive Oil Marinade

Makes 1 cup

*⅔ cup extra-virgin olive oil*

*⅓ cup red wine vinegar*

*2 cloves garlic, minced*

*2 teaspoons minced parsley*

*1 teaspoon grated lemon zest*

*½ teaspoon fine sea salt*

*Freshly ground black pepper to taste*

*Extra-virgin olive oil and good red wine vinegar are the essential ingredients for dressing salad greens. They also combine with herbs and spices to make marinades for meats, fowl, and fish. I prepare marinades in glass jars and keep the mixtures in my refrigerator. Bring the marinade to room temperature before using.*

Place all the ingredients in a jar, cap it, and shake well. Leave the marinade at room temperature for several hours before using to marinate meats, poultry, fish, or vegetables.

# Pinzimonio

## Raw Vegetables with Extra-Virgin Olive Oil

*Extra-virgin olive oil is a central ingredient in everything I cook, even dessert (see* torta di cioccolata d'olio d'oliva, *page 118), but in this "recipe" for* pinzimonio *(a bowl of crunchy raw vegetables), it is the* main ingredient.

Make an artistic arrangement in a bowl with tall stalks of celery and carrots with their green tops attached. Add thick slices of red, yellow, and orange sweet peppers. Tuck in chunks of fennel and long sticks of zucchini along with some crunchy radishes and cucumbers.

Pour some extra-virgin olive oil into a bowl and let everyone help themselves by dipping the vegetables in the oil. You may want to have some salt and pepper on the table, too. I like to accompany the *pinzimonio* with crusty bread and a dish of assorted olives.

# Torta di Cioccolata all'Olio d'Oliva

## Chocolate Olive-Oil Cake

3 cups unbleached
all-purpose flour

2 cups sugar

6 tablespoons cocoa
(Perugina, if possible)

2 teaspoons baking soda

½ teaspoon salt

¾ cup extra-virgin
olive oil

2 tablespoons
white vinegar

1 tablespoon
vanilla extract

2 cups cold water

FROSTING

Two 8-ounce packages
Philadelphia Lite
Cream Cheese
at room temperature

3½ to 4 cups
confectioners' sugar

*Even cakes taste better made with olive oil. This dense super-chocolaty cake is so moist that it keeps well for a week in the refrigerator. But I can say with certainty that it will not last that long. As an alternative, the batter can be poured into cupcake pans for smaller versions. This cake freezes well.*

Preheat the oven to 350° F.

Butter and flour two 9-inch cake pans and set aside.

Mix the flour, sugar, cocoa, baking soda, and salt together in a large bowl. With a hand mixer on low speed beat in the oil, vinegar, vanilla, and water until smooth. Pour the mixture into the prepared pans.

Bake for 30 minutes, or until a cake skewer inserted in the center comes out clean. Do not overbake. The cake should be firm to the touch.

Place the cake pans on cooling racks and cool for 15 to 20 minutes, then remove the cakes from the pans to cool completely.

To make the frosting: Beat the cream cheese in a bowl until smooth. Gradually add enough sugar to make a smooth frosting that is not runny. Stir in the cinnamon oil.

Frost the cake layers when cool and sprinkle the crystallized sugar over the top. Cut into wedges to serve.

*Variation: If you are making cupcakes with this recipe, use a pastry bag with a star tip to pipe icing onto the tops, then sprinkle the icing with sugar.*

*¼ teaspoon cinnamon oil or 1 tablespoon almond extract*

**Crystallized white sugar for sprinkling on top**

# Pietro's Garden

*Frittatina di Verdure* (Vegetable Frittata)

*I* cook from instinct, not from recipes. So in my mental kitchen I am always scheming about new ways to present food. If I am in my garden, I think about clever ways to use an army of zucchini or bushelfuls of plum tomatoes. If I am in Italy, I study the foods in the markets and dream about how I would prepare them. If I am driving in the Umbrian countryside and spot a gorgeous vegetable garden—as I did one day when the television crew and I were on the lookout for great footage that would capture the real Umbria—my mind races with new ideas.

*A garden is a joy at any age, as Pietro knows.*

One day as we drove through the town of Branca on our way to Gubbio, a beautiful patchwork quilt of a vegetable garden, complete with an elderly gentleman sporting a tweed beret and vigorously hoeing the rows, came into view. I looked at the crew, and we all said, "That's it. Let's do it!"

We swarmed down the hill like locusts, hoping to capture the essence of an Umbrian home garden (with permission, of course). *"Sono Marianna,"* I called out, and introduced the rest of the crew to Pietro Cardoni, who was leaning on his rake and seemed bewildered to see a band of Americans in his backyard. He was soft-spoken and almost meditative in his demeanor. I told him in my halting Italian why we were in Umbria and asked if he would allow us to film him at work in the garden. He motioned us into a luscious area of green plants all happily thriving under the Umbrian sun. One by one he pointed out the names of the plants—here tomatoes, there peppers, and so on.

"What do you do with all these vegetables?" I asked.

"My sister-in-law, Pirarina, cooks them," he said with a laugh. "I just plant them for the table and for the fun of it."

"Is it true that most Italians have gardens?"

"Yes. Wherever there is a patch of land, the Italians will plant because not everyone lives near a city where they can go to the markets to get vegetables. Most of us live in small towns, so we must think of ourselves."

Looking around at the great expanse of land, I could see his point. No *supermercati* here!

Soon our presence brought the rest of the family members outside to help in the garden. There was brother Carlo and his wife, Pirarina. They took up their rakes and watering cans, and headed down the rows, eager to show us everything. Carlo was proud of the potato patch. Pirarina could not possibly cook without her beloved onions and parsley. I asked what her favorite vegetables were and how she cooked them. *"Basta, le verdure miste, olio d'oliva, prezzemolo, aglio e cosi si fa qualcosa da mangiare."* That's how I do it, too, I told her—just vegetables, olive oil, parsley, and garlic. She tapped me on the shoulder to remind me that I must use Umbrian olive oil!

It didn't seem as if hours had gone by when I looked at my watch. We had spent the day gathering invaluable footage and learning the secrets of a good garden: *"Pazienza"* (patience), Pietro cautioned, and a good back; God and nature will take care of the rest. And he reminded us, "Every garden needs a dead man." I wasn't quite sure what he meant and asked him to explain. "A garden needs constant watching, someone who is always there." Enough said.

It was time to go. I left truly inspired by the reverence and care that Pietro and his family showed for the land and how every inch of space was utilized—good lessons to take home to my own garden.

# Frittatina di Verdure

## Vegetable Frittata

Serves 4

*Pietro Cardoni's Umbrian garden had everything I needed to make this vegetable frittatina. The beauty of this "recipe" is that it allows you to use a variety of your favorite vegetables, resulting in a tasty omelet whose flavor is lifted by a balsamic vinegar dressing. Instead of folding the vegetables into the egg mixture, they are cooked separately to retain their al dente texture and then placed on top of the frittata along with some aged ricotta cheese (ricotta salata) and peppery arugula. A great luncheon idea. Other vegetables could include small broccoli or cauliflower florets, asparagus, sweet peppers, summer squash, and sugar snap peas. Get inspired!*

To make the dressing: Combine the vinegar, olive oil, and salt in a jar and set aside.

Fill a plastic bag with ice cubes and 3 cups of water and set aside.

Cook the pancetta in a 10-inch nonstick sauté pan until crispy. Drain the pancetta on paper towels and set aside.

Fill a 1-quart saucepan with 3 cups of water. Bring to a boil and add 1 teaspoon of salt. Cook the beans, uncovered, until *al dente* (just tender); they should retain their crunch. Remove the beans with a slotted spoon and transfer them to the bag with the ice water. (This stops the cooking process and allows the beans to retain their vibrant color.) Leave the beans in the bag for 3 or 4 minutes, then remove them with a slotted spoon and let them drain on paper towels. Add the potatoes to the boiling water and

### DRESSING

*⅓ cup balsamic vinegar*

*½ cup extra-virgin olive oil*

*Salt to taste*

*4 ounces chunk pancetta, cut into cubes*

*8 ounces green beans, julienned*

*2 small new potatoes, peeled and cubed*

*4 small carrots, peeled and cubed*

*2 small zucchini, cubed*

*4 eggs*

*¼ cup minced parsley*

*¼ teaspoon salt*

*4 tablespoons extra-virgin olive oil*

*2 slightly green tomatoes, thinly sliced*

½ cup shredded arugula

4 ounces ricotta salata
   cheese, cut from the
   wedge into small,
   chiplike pieces

cook until *al dente;* remove the potatoes with a slotted spoon and set aside. Cook the carrots in the same water and drain them in the same way as the green beans.

Whisk the eggs in a bowl with the parsley and ¼ teaspoon of salt. Set aside.

Heat the oil in a 10-inch nonstick skillet. Pour in the egg mixture and cook until it is set. Slide the *frittatina* onto a serving dish and cut into 4 wedges. Arrange the tomato slices over the top of the *frittatina,* then the beans, potatoes, carrots, zucchini, arugula, and pancetta.

Pour the dressing over the top and sprinkle the cheese over the dressing. Serve immediately.

*Variation: If you cannot have eggs in your diet, use EggBeaters, substituting 1 cup for the 4 eggs.*

# A Trip to the Norcineria

*Braciolette di Maiale alla Spoletina* (Pork Chops Spoleto Style)

*Salsiccia Fresca* (Fresh Sausage)

*Salsicce all'Uve* (Sweet Pork Sausages with Grapes)

*Scaloppine di Maiale in Salsa Verde* (Pork Scallops in Green Sauce)

*Who could resist the artisanal products of Umbria?*

What would the region of Umbria be without its *porchetta, salsicce, prosciutti,* and *salame locale*? These are all pork products, and along with creamy lentils and black truffles they are the major foods of Umbrian cuisine. Pork *(maiale)* is a gastronomic symbol of the region, recognized for its superior quality worldwide. *Porchetta alla griglia* (grilled pork), *allo spiedo* (on the spit), and *insaccati* (cured pork products stuffed into natural casings) are made in Umbria by experts called *norcini,* or pork butchers. The tradition dates back to the seventeenth century in the rugged mountain town of Norcia, located in the southeastern part of Umbria. Norcia is an ancient Sabine settlement whose name means fortune, which seems appropriate for one of Italy's culinary capitals; anyone who enjoys the delicious pork from here knows why.

A stop in Norcia is a must for anyone serious about Umbrian foods. The minute you walk into a *norcineria* (pork butcher's shop), the soothing smell of naturally spiced, cured meats overtakes your senses. Cured pork includes some of my favorites, such as *la coppa,* which is cooked and air-dried boneless pork from the neck area of the pig that is stuffed into a casing; there are stacks of spicy and mild versions of *salumi* (cured meats), which make great lunch fare or an antipasto, and there are the *prosciutti,* the local salt and air-dried hams that dangle from the ceiling on long strings. There are huge cooked sausages of finely ground pork called *mortadella;* blended with spices, it is totally different from the famous mortadella of Bologna that is studded with pistachio nuts or cubes of creamy white lard. You might be tempted to call it baloney, but it bears no resemblance to that placid cold cut from home. Forget cold cuts altogether. In Italy these are cured meats that have received careful attention in their preparation, and only the finest pork and seasonings are used; no artificial color or flavors ever come into contact with *salumi.*

Not to be slighted are the noncured fresh pork products ready for the grill, such as *salsicce* (fresh sausages) and juicy pork chops. Looking at the coiled sausages reminds me of my own sausage-making (page 132) and how superior homemade can be to the grocery store variety. Plus, I know what's in it—no preservatives and no artificial anything!

The work of the *norcini* is laborious, and if you come to Norcia in the wintertime when pigs are butchered, you will see that nothing is wasted. All parts of the pig are used, including the blood, which is cooked into something called *sanguinacci*, or blood pudding. The innards of the animal, including the heart, liver, and intestines, are made into *padellaccia*, which is chopped together and cooked quickly in a skillet with olive oil, spices, and wine.

A trip to the *norcineria* is a reminder that this artisanal craft has been passed down for centuries by *norcini* who have put this mountain land squarely at the center of Umbrian gastronomy.

# *Braciolette di Maiale alla Spoletina*

## Pork Chops Spoleto Style

Serves 4

*N*ot *too far from Norcia is the city of Spoleto, where each year the festival* Dei Due Mondi *is held, attracting music lovers from all over the world. As in other parts of Umbria, the food here is defined by its fine extra-virgin olive oil and pork products. These savory and easy-to-prepare pork chops are characteristic of the style of cooking called* alla Spoletina, *featuring local olives, olive oil, and wine.*

Use a chef's knife to mince the olives together into a fine paste. Transfer the paste to a small bowl and set aside.

Dry the pork chops well on both sides with paper towels. This will help ensure that they brown well. Drop them into a heavy-duty paper bag with the flour, salt, and pepper. Close the bag and shake to coat the chops. Remove them from the bag, shaking off the excess flour, and place them on a dish.

Heat the olive oil in a sauté pan large enough to hold the chops in 1 layer. When the oil begins to shimmer and smoke, add the chops, lower the heat to medium, and brown them well on both sides. Pour in ¾ cup of the wine and allow most of it to evaporate. Remove the chops to a dish and keep them warm. Stir the olive paste and the remaining wine into the pan, and scrape up any bits clinging to the bottom of the pan. Pour the sauce over the chops and serve immediately.

*6 oil-cured Kalamata olives, pitted*

*6 oil-cured Cerignola or other green olives, pitted*

*4 center-cut pork chops*

*¼ cup flour*

*¼ teaspoon salt*

*Freshly ground coarse black pepper to taste*

*3 tablespoons extra-virgin olive oil*

*1 cup dry white wine such as Orvieto Classico*

# Salsiccia Fresca

## Fresh Sausage

Makes 5 pounds

*1 package
natural hog casings
(available in your
grocery store's
deli section)*

*5 pounds boneless pork
butt, ground once
on coarse and
once on medium*

*2 tablespoons
coarse salt,
or more to taste*

*2 tablespoons
coarsely ground
pepper, or more to
taste*

*3 tablespoons
fennel seeds*

*There is nothing like homemade pork sausage, the kind I remember
from my childhood when pork had more fat—and more flavor. Today's
pork presents a dilemma; it is too lean, in my opinion, and usually
turns out dry and tasteless. Don't despair. This is my standby recipe,
and I think you'll find plenty of that homemade flavor. All you need is a
good butcher to grind the pork for you, and a good thumb!*

Soak 4 casings in a bowl in several changes of cold water to get rid
of the salt. Cut the casings with a scissors into 12- to 14-inch
lengths. Keep the rest of the casings in the refrigerator; they will
last several weeks.

Slip one end of the casing opening onto the throat of a sausage
funnel and slide the casing all the way up onto the funnel, leaving
about 3 inches free at the end. Tie a knot at the end.

In a bowl, combine the pork with all the seasonings. Test for
taste by frying a small amount in a sauté pan; add more seasonings
if you wish.

Push small amounts of the pork through the casing with your
thumb and continue filling the casing all the way, leaving about 2
inches free at the top. Slip the top of the casing off the funnel and
tie a knot. Use a fork or toothpick to poke holes all over the sausage;
this will allow fat to escape during cooking (see directions for cooking sausage in the following recipe).

Continue making sausage until all the pork mixture is used. Well-wrapped sausages can be frozen for up to 1 year.

*Variation:* *For hot sausage add 2 tablespoons or more of hot red pepper flakes when preparing the sausage mixture.*

# Salsicce all'Uve

## Sweet Pork Sausages with Grapes

Serves 4

*1 pound homemade
or store-bought
sweet Italian sausage*

*1 tablespoon
olive oil (optional)*

*2 cups seedless grapes,
cut in half*

*T*wo products of Umbria, grapes and pork, make this sausage dish delicious and a snap to prepare. I like to make my own pork sausage (page 132), but already prepared is fine, too. Look for lean sweet sausage; the hot variety is not as good with sugary grapes.

Poke the sausages with a fork and put them in a sauté pan with ½ cup of water. Cook the sausages, uncovered, over medium heat until the sausages turn a uniform gray color. Drain off the water. Allow the sausages to brown in their own fat, turning them once or twice. (They should finish cooking in about 15 minutes.) If they are very lean, add the olive oil. Five minutes before the sausage is cooked, add the grapes to the pan.

Serve very hot.

# Scaloppine di Maiale in Salsa Verde

## Pork Scallops in Green Sauce

Serves 6

*Salsa verde, green sauce (page 144), is the secret to the success of this boneless pork cutlet dish; without the sauce, the meat is rather bland. Use thin slices of pork for the scaloppine. To keep the sauce looking green, drop the parsley and basil leaves into boiling water for 30 seconds, then drain and dry them before making the sauce. The sauce is also good served over pasta or mixed into risotto.*

**4 tablespoons extra-virgin olive oil**

**1½ pounds thinly sliced (about ¼ inch thick) pork cutlet**

**½ cup sliced mushrooms (button, cremini, portobello, or porcini)**

**1 cup salsa verde (page 144)**

Pour 2 tablespoons of the olive oil into a large sauté pan and heat until the oil begins to shimmer. Brown the pork pieces, a few at a time, on both sides, adding additional oil if the pan gets dry. As the pieces brown, remove them to a dish. Stir in the mushrooms, adding a little more oil if necessary, and cook over medium heat until they exude their liquid and begin to brown. Return the cutlets to the pan, lower the heat, and stir in the *salsa verde*. Gently mix all the ingredients until hot. Transfer the pork and sauce to a platter and serve immediately.

# Simple Sauces

*Ragù Umbro* (Umbrian *Ragù* Sauce)

*Salsa d'Acciughe* (Anchovy Sauce)

*Salsa Ghiotta* (Drip Pan Sauce)

*Salsa Verde* (Green Sauce)

*Sugo Finto* (False Sauce)

*Salsa ai Tartufi Neri* (Black Truffle Sauce)

*U*mbria's lifestyle is reflected in its cooking. Fresh quality ingredients, seasonal flavors, few adornments, and attention to tradition pretty much sizes up my observations of the food. Umbrian flavors are not masked in a minestrone soup of ingredients. Instead, minimalist cooking prevails, and by that I mean using just a few ingredients to create good flavor that complements a dish but does not overpower it.

This is also true of sauces. The two signature sauces in Umbria are *salsa ghiotta* and *salsa ai tartufi neri* (page 144). *Salsa ghiotta* is nothing more than a sauce made from the pan drippings of meat roasting on a spit. In fact, the word *ghiotta* refers to the drip pan placed beneath spit-roasting meats to catch the flavorful juices. Wine, vinegar, lemon juice, sage leaves, and black olives are often added to the drip pan. I have given you a version in this chapter. Other sauces are found throughout this book.

*Salsa ai tartufi neri*, black truffle sauce, is probably the most exotic and unique because of its earthy, woodsy flavor, and because it is an uncooked sauce in which thin shavings of truffle are steeped in warmed extra-virgin olive oil. What a simple preparation—but what a complex flavor. Another classic sauce is *sugo finto,* "false sauce," so-called because it is nearly meatless and economical to make. *Salsa verde* means green sauce and is made most frequently with fresh parsley and dense extra-virgin olive oil. It is popular on grilled meats and vegetables. *Salsa alla perugina* is a sauce that features chicken livers.

*Ragù* sauce immediately brings to mind a thick meat sauce, forgotten on the stove and simmered for hours, as is the custom in the region of Emilia-Romagna. In Umbria, *ragù* sauces are not as popular and often include the addition of black truffles at the end of the cooking.

All these sauces celebrate the elements that define Umbrian cooking: extra-virgin olive oil; meat products such as pork; black truffles; herbs such as sage, parsley, and rosemary; and wine—plus the ingenuity of the cook to use them in creative ways in order to maximize the flavors found in the Umbrian kitchen.

# Ragù Umbro

## Umbrian *Ragù* Sauce

Makes about 5½ cups

Ragù *sauces are those made with meat and cooked for a long time, and they differ from region to region throughout Italy. Umbria ragùs are not as common as other types of sauces, but here is one that is easy to make and essential to the* parmigiana di cipolla *recipe on page 53; it is also good on a short cut of pasta such as rigatoni or ziti. The ubiquitous ingredient is shaved black truffle, which is added at the end of the cooking, but of course this is optional. The other unusual ingredient is nutmeg, which gives a subtle hint of sweetness and spiciness to the sauce. See Mail Order Sources on page 199 for black truffle sources.*

Melt the butter in a sauté pan over medium heat and cook the carrot, celery, and onion until they are soft. Stir in the pork and beef, and brown well. Stir in the ham and cook 1 minute more. Raise the heat to high, pour in the wine, and allow it to evaporate. Stir in the tomatoes, salt, pepper, and nutmeg. Lower the heat and simmer the sauce, covered, for 35 minutes. Uncover the pan and shave the black truffle over the top. Cover the pan and allow the truffle to permeate the *ragù* for 2 or 3 minutes without turning the heat back on.

**1 tablespoon butter**

**1 large carrot, scraped and diced**

**2 ribs celery, diced**

**1 medium onion, diced**

**12 ounces ground pork**

**4 ounces ground beef**

**4 ounces cooked ham, diced**

**⅔ cup dry white wine**

**4 large plum tomatoes, seeded and diced**

**½ teaspoon salt**

**Freshly ground coarse black pepper to taste**

**¼ teaspoon nutmeg**

**1 small black truffle (optional)**

# Salsa d'Acciughe

## Anchovy Sauce

Makes about ¾ cup

*4 anchovy fillets, packed in olive oil, drained, and minced*

*1 tablespoon capers in salt, rinsed, patted dry, and minced*

*1 large clove garlic, minced*

*⅔ cup extra-virgin olive oil*

*Juice of 1 large lemon*

*4 mint leaves, minced*

*Fine sea salt to taste*

*Freshly ground coarse black pepper to taste*

*This is the quickest sauce you will ever make: It needs no cooking! Be sure to use good imported anchovies packed in olive oil. This is a good basting sauce for fish; it is tangy brushed on roasted tomatoes or eggplant, and it is flavorful enough to dress a half pound of pasta.*

Place all the ingredients in a screw-top jar and shake well. Let marinate for several hours at room temperature before using.

# Salsa Ghiotta

## Drip Pan Sauce

Makes approximately 1 cup

*According to tradition, wild game is cooked on the spit in Umbrian kitchens. The meat is brushed frequently with a sauce made from the drippings kept underneath the spit in the* ghiotta, *or juice pan. Here is an adaptation of the recipe made without pan drippings. Use this sauce to baste chicken, pheasant, game hens, and meats as they cook on the grill or in the oven.*

Mix all the ingredients together.

½ *cup dry red wine*

¼ *cup extra-virgin olive oil*

*6 sage leaves, minced*

*1 tablespoon minced capers*

*2 cloves garlic, minced*

*1 tablespoon minced rosemary needles*

*Fine sea salt to taste*

*Freshly ground coarse black pepper to taste*

*1 anchovy in salt, rinsed and chopped*

# Salsa Verde

## Green Sauce

Makes about 1¼ cups

*16 tablespoons (2 sticks) unsalted butter at room temperature*

*4 cloves garlic, minced*

*½ cup coarsely chopped walnuts*

*1½ cups packed parsley leaves*

*½ cup packed fresh basil leaves, without stems*

*½ teaspoon fine sea salt*

*Freshly ground black pepper to taste*

*3 to 4 tablespoons extra-virgin olive oil*

Salsa verde, or green sauce, is made with fresh parsley, basil, extra-virgin olive oil, salt, and pepper. It is a great partner to grilled eggplant or zucchini, and is equally as good as a sauce for spaghetti. I like it on grilled fish and mixed into risotto. It is best to make this in a food processor.

Place all the ingredients except the olive oil in the bowl of a food processor fitted with a steel blade. Process until smooth. With the motor running, pour just enough of the oil through the feed tube to create a thick, creamy, fluid sauce.

Transfer the sauce to a jar and store in the refrigerator. Use within a week. As the sauce sits, it tends to become brown if not airtight.

# Sugo Finto

## False Sauce

Makes 2 cups

*He*re is an intriguing name for a sauce, sugo finto, *meaning "false sauce" because it is nearly meatless and economical to make. You probably have the ingredients to make it in your refrigerator. Use meaty tomatoes and drop them in a pan of boiling water for a minute or two to loosen their skins, making them easy to peel. This sauce is good on short cuts of pasta, such as ziti.*

Mince together the onion, carrot, and celery with a chef's knife.

Heat the olive oil and butter in a saucepan, and when the butter has melted, stir in the minced vegetables. Cook until they begin to soften. Stir in the ham and cook until it begins to brown. Stir in the tomatoes, basil, salt, and pepper. Cover the pan and simmer the sauce for 10 minutes.

*1 small onion,
  peeled and quartered*

*1 carrot, scraped
  and quartered*

*1 rib celery, quartered*

*2 tablespoons extra-
  virgin olive oil*

*2 tablespoons
  unsalted butter*

*3 slices boiled ham,
  minced*

*8 large, ripe plum
  tomatoes, peeled,
  seeded, and chopped*

*3 basil leaves*

*Fine sea salt to taste*

*Freshly ground coarse
  black pepper to taste*

# Salsa ai Tartufi Neri

## Black Truffle Sauce

Makes ⅔ cup

*2 fresh black truffles
or 2 jarred
black truffles*

*⅔ cup extra-virgin
olive oil*

*2 cloves garlic, minced*

*½ teaspoon salt*

*Black truffles, extra-virgin olive oil, and a couple of cloves of garlic are all the ingredients necessary to make a classic black truffle sauce. Purists will tell you that truffles must never be truly cooked, only warmed in the olive oil to release its distinct flavor. Purists will also tell you that a truffle shaver is necessary to shave the truffles as thin as tissue paper, while others maintain that the truffles should be grated for maximum flavor. Either way the sauce is exquisite.*

Clean the truffles with a brush if they are dirty. Slice them very thin using a cheese grater or truffle shaver, or grate them if you prefer. If using jarred truffles, thinly slice them with a knife since they will be softer. Set aside.

Heat the olive oil in a sauté pan, stir in the garlic, and cook just until it softens. Add the truffles and salt and steep the truffles over very low heat for 2 or 3 minutes. Use immediately on pasta or as a topping for crusty bread.

# Straight from the Hearth

*Brustengo* (Gubbian Flat Bread)

*Torta sul Testo* (Umbrian Griddle-Baked Flat Bread)

*Tortina di Prosciutto* (Prosciutto Pie)

*Coniglio in Porchetta* (Terra-cotta-Cooked Rabbit, Gubbian Style)

*Antipasto need not be complicated, just complementary.*

*B*read is considered a sacred food by all Italians, and one that is never wasted. Left-over pieces are put into soups, made into bread crumbs, crumbled into bread salads, turned into bread gnocchi, mixed into stuffings, and, finely ground, used to dust cake pans. Bread was suste-nance for shepherds spending long days with their flocks in the pasturelands; it was fuel for the Roman armies, precious cargo on sailing ships, the symbol of life for Christians, and often the reason that wars were waged.

Umbrian bread takes many forms, many of which are saltless, a custom from the sixteenth century when the Pope imposed a salt tax, which the citizenry refused to pay.

No matter which region of Italy one focuses on regarding bread, it is safe to say that the first breads were primitive: flat-as-a-pancake unleavened breads that were nothing more than wild wheat flour and water made into a dough and cooked on hot stones.

Later, around 400 B.C., according to archaeological evidence, yeast breads were developed in Egypt. As civilization advanced, yeast breads were baked directly on the hearth; for example, *focca-cia*—which takes its name from *focolare,* meaning hearth—is a flat bread found in all regions of Italy that goes by many different names.

Today when you step into a *panificio* (bread shop) in Italy, you will encounter flat breads from all over Italy, from Venetian *fogasse* to the *piadina* of Ravenna, to the rustic *brustengo,* the fried bread of Gubbio.

As I discovered while studying Umbrian cooking in Perugia, Umbrian flat breads are unassuming, nonfussy breads meant to go it alone or with just a drizzle of extra-virgin olive oil and a few herbs scattered on top; or they might be flavored with crispy bits of prosciutto or cut into wedges and stuffed with bitter greens like the *torta sul testo* on page 152.

# Brustengo

## Gubbian Flat Bread

*A pitch-black skillet is what chef Fina uses in the kitchen of the Bossone Garden restaurant when she makes* brustengo, *the fried flat bread of Gubbio. If you make the batter ahead of time, it will thicken slightly; it should be pourable, like pancake batter, so thin it down before you use it, if necessary. Serve the bread warm as is or with prosciutto, dried sausage, and olives for an antipasto.*

**4 cups unbleached all-purpose flour**

**3½ cups water**

**1 teaspoon salt**

**Vegetable oil for frying**

Mix the flour, water, and salt together in a bowl. I like to use one with a pourable spout.

Pour the oil to a depth of ½ inch into a 10-inch heavy-duty skillet or frying pan and heat until hot. Test the hotness of the oil by dropping a small dribble of batter into the skillet; if it browns and bubbles immediately, the oil is hot enough. I keep a candy thermometer in the oil to make sure it is at 375° F. Pour or scoop and spread about a cupful of the batter into the oil, and when the bread begins to brown around the edges, flip it over carefully to brown the other side. Use a slotted spoon to remove the bread and allow it to drain on paper towels.

Use up all the batter in the same way. Depending on the size of your pan, you should be able to get at least 10 to 12 rounds.

# Torta sul Testo

## Umbrian Griddle-Baked Flat Bread

Makes 6 rounds or 12 small sandwiches

FILLING

*20 ounces fresh spinach, stemmed and rinsed well*

*2 tablespoons extra-virgin olive oil*

*4 ounces prosciutto, diced*

*Freshly ground coarse black pepper to taste*

DOUGH

*3½ cups unbleached all-purpose flour*

*1 teaspoon baking soda*

*1 large egg*

*3 tablespoons extra-virgin olive oil*

*6 tablespoons grated pecorino cheese*

*Warm water as needed*

*Flat bread cooked on a dry skillet is reminiscent of some of the first unleavened breads. In Umbria this has evolved into* torta sul testo, *or bread baked in earthenware. I use a dry electric skillet. A stovetop griddle will work well, too.* Torta sul testo *is often served with a stuffing of bitter greens such as spinach or broccoli rabe, or served warm without a stuffing, accompanied by pecorino cheese and oil-cured olives for an antipasto.*

Cook the spinach, without the addition of any water, in a 2-quart pot, covered, about 3 or 4 minutes, or just until it wilts. Transfer the spinach to a colander and squeeze it dry with a wooden spoon or let it cool and squeeze it dry with your hands. On a cutting board chop the spinach fine and set aside.

Heat the olive oil in a sauté pan. Add the prosciutto and cook until it begins to brown and crisp. Stir in the spinach and a good grinding of pepper, and mix well. Set aside.

To make the dough: Mix the flour and baking soda together in a bowl. In another bowl, beat the egg, olive oil, and cheese together. Add this to the flour mixture and mix with your hands to obtain a soft dough. Add warm water, 2 tablespoons at a time, if the dough seems dry. It should feel soft and pliable. Knead the dough on a floured surface for 5 minutes, or until smooth and elastic. Let it rest, covered, for 10 minutes. Divide the dough into 6 pieces and roll each piece into a 6-inch circle. Set the circles aside on a floured surface.

Heat a cast-iron griddle, frying pan, or electric frying pan until hot. Prick the circles all over with a fork. This will help keep the rounds flat as they cook. Use a small glass to make overlapping circle designs on each piece. These marks are decorative. Place 1 or 2 circles on the hot pan; do not cook more than 2 at a time. Cook until they have browned slightly on the bottom, about 3 or 4 minutes, then turn them over and brown on the other side.

Transfer the circles to a wire rack to cool completely.

Divide the spinach mixture among 3 of the circles. Top with the remaining 3 circles. With a knife cut each into 4 wedges to make 12. Serve warm.

# Tortina di Prosciutto

## Prosciutto Pie

Serves 8 to 10

*1½ teaspoons
active dry yeast*

*3¼ cups warm milk
(110° F)*

*2 large eggs,
lightly beaten*

*6 tablespoons
unsalted butter, melted*

*¼ teaspoon fine sea salt*

*1 cup grated
Parmigiano-Reggiano
cheese*

*3¼ to 3½ cups
unbleached
all-purpose flour*

*4 ounces prosciutto,
finely diced*

*1 tablespoon
minced rosemary*

*Faithful to the tradition of Umbrian flat breads, this prosciutto pie comes from the Hotel Grifone's cooking school in Perugia. It is a yeast bread but is made in a rectangular pan and cut into squares. It is a great antipasto for a party and is best eaten hot. I like it teamed with warm chickpea and farro salad (page 86). I have taken a few liberties with the recipe, adding rosemary and more cheese. The dough can be made effortlessly in a food processor.*

In a small bowl, dissolve the yeast in the milk. Set aside.

Mix the eggs, butter, salt, and cheese together in a large bowl. Stir in the yeast mixture. Gradually add the flour, mixing it with your hands until a ball of dough forms that does not stick to your hands; you may not need all the flour.

Knead the dough on a lightly floured surface until soft and smooth. Place the dough in an oiled bowl and cover tightly with plastic wrap. Let it rise for 2 hours in a warm but not hot area, about 75° F.

Preheat the oven to 350° F. Lightly grease a 15 × 12-inch baking pan.

Punch down the dough with your hands and put it on a work surface. Flatten the dough and sprinkle the prosciutto and rosemary over the top. Fold the dough on itself to enclose the ingredients and knead for 3 or 4 minutes to evenly distribute the ingredients.

Roll the dough into a 15 × 12-inch rectangle and place it on the prepared baking sheet. Bake the *tortina* until golden brown, about 20 to 25 minutes.

Cut into small squares and serve hot.

# Coniglio in Porchetta

## Terra-cotta-Cooked Rabbit, Gubbian Style

Serves 4

*3 tablespoons
extra-virgin olive oil*

*½ pound sweet Italian
sausage, casing
removed*

*2 medium baking
potatoes, peeled
and diced*

*3 cloves garlic,
thinly sliced*

*1½ cups finely chopped
fennel tops*

*One 3½-pound whole
rabbit or chicken,
rinsed well and dried*

*½ cup dry white wine*

*The day I made what seemed like a small mountain of* brustengo *(page 151) in chef Fina's kitchen, I also cooked with chef Walter Potenza who lives in Providence, Rhode Island, and who travels to Umbria each year to teach cooking classes in Gubbio. He believes that a chef must conform to the clock of nature and use only the finest ingredients of the season and prepare them in the most authentic way. I spent the day with him cooking Umbrian specialties, including the classic Gubbian dish of succulent, slow-oven-cooked rabbit* (coniglio in porchetta), *for which he uses a terra-cotta pot that is presoaked in water for fifteen minutes. Terra-cotta helps to maintain moisture as the meat cooks. Lacking that, use an earthenware baking dish. The mild flavor of the rabbit is balanced nicely by the savory sausage and fennel stuffing. Chicken can be substituted for rabbit.*

Preheat oven to 350 F.

Heat 1 tablespoon of the olive oil in a sauté pan; add all the ingredients except the rabbit or chicken, and stir from time to time until the sausage is no longer red. When the mixture is cool enough to handle, stuff the filling into the cavity of the rabbit or chicken; do not pack it too tightly or it will spill out in the cooking process. If there is any filling left after stuffing the rabbit, put it into a separate baking dish and cook it along with the meat.

Pour the remaining olive oil into the base of the terra-cotta pot and add the rabbit. Cover the pot and cook for 35 to 40 minutes, basting the meat with the wine and the cooking juices that accumulate in the pan. Uncover the pot, raise the heat to 375° F and cook 45 minutes longer, or until the rabbit is fork-tender and the liquid is almost completely absorbed.

Serve the rabbit cut into pieces accompanied by some of the stuffing and pan juices and a vegetable like swiss chard, green beans, broccoli rabe, or broccoli.

# The Fishermen and the Lace Makers

*Regina in Porchetta* (Carp with Rosemary and Fennel)

*Tegamaccio* (Lago Trasimeno Fish Stew)

*Trota alla Griglia* (Grilled Trout)

*Searching for eels on Lago Trasimeno*

*I*sola Maggiore, or Greater Island, is soothed on all sides by placid Lago Trasimeno, one of the largest lakes in Italy and the largest in landlocked Umbria. By all accounts Lago Trasimeno played a very large role in the history of the region. Back in 217 B.C., the Carthaginian leader Hannibal, warring against the Romans, was able to swoop down with his troops and catch the Roman army completely off guard, massacring over sixteen thousand legionnaires near the lakefront town of Tuoro sul Trasimeno. That was enough of a historic reason for me to visit. The other was to see the lace makers on Isola Maggiore. So on a cold and drizzly day, *come Dio ha commandato* (as God commanded), I took the fifteen-minute trip on the *traghetto* (ferry) to the island of Tuoro sul Trasimeno. People say that the lake is slowly drying up, but this was hard to believe as I looked out over the vastness of its baby blue waters from the back of the ferry. Along the shoreline I could see a panorama of hills dotted with olive groves and thick stands of cypress and poplar trees. It was a beautiful trip, and I felt transported to another world as I stepped onto the pier.

I was eager to learn all I could about lace-making which is so important here. It seemed eerily quiet as I walked toward the center of the island. The rain had dampened the spirits of would-be sightseers—all the better to have the whole island to myself! I was chilled to the bone and spotted a bar where I could get an espresso. I struck up a conversation with the three bar owners. "Isn't this a good day to catch fish?" "Signora," they said in unison, "the fishing industry is nearly dead here, and there are only seven fishermen left on Isola Maggiore." This was the worst news I could have heard, and suddenly my mood mirrored that of the weather. "I want to speak to a fisherman," I told them, and they rolled their eyes and motioned with their hands for me to ask at the information center.

The little booth was not far away, and as I made my way there, I spotted a tall man pulling a net from a boat. *"Scusi,"* I said, trying to get his attention and feeling a bit guilty about interrupting his meditative work. His name was Rolando, and, yes, he had been a fisherman for fifty years. But now it was lean times, he told me; the fish were hard to come by. He was kind enough to use his nets to pull up some eels *(anguille)*, one of the delicacies of Umbrian cooking. They slithered and slid in his bucket, and I asked him how he cooked them. He gave me his favorite options: *allo spiedo,* on a spit on the grill, or in a typical Umbrian fish stew called *tegamaccio.* Many people shudder at the thought of eating eel, but it is a delicious, delicate-tasting fish, and by local custom the eels from Lago Trasimeno are sent to the Vatican so the Pope can enjoy them, too.

"What other fish are still in the lake?" I asked. *"Ma certo,"* he replied. "There is the *regina,* the carp, the queen of fish—so-called because of its size. These are grilled with fennel and lemon. There is pike [*luccio*], tench [*tinca*], perch [*persico*], and catfish [*pesce gatto*]."

Thanking him for his time, I asked where I could find the famous lace makers, and Rolando pointed me in their direction. "Go to via Guglielmi, a single street that was home in the past to the fishermen of Isola Maggiore and to the seven now remaining. You can still see fishing nets drying out in the sun." Once I found it, it was hard to miss the rows of elderly women sitting on hardback chairs up and down the street, bent over what seemed to be very tedious work: the intricate handcraft of lace-making. Around them were displayed delicate spider-web designs of their art, from shawls to bureau scarves to pocket handkerchiefs that are too exquisite, in my mind, ever to touch a running nose.

I stopped to talk to a woman named Maria who had been making lace since she was six years old. She told me the reason that Isola Maggiore was so famous for lace-making. In the nineteenth century Elena Tasetti de Santis started a school here where the fishermen's daughters could learn how to make *pizzo Irlando* (Irish lace). Since girls were already skilled at mending their family's fishing nets, it was not difficult to teach them the fine art of lace-making. Watching Maria's skilled, withered hands work the very fine cotton thread with the crochet hook was like watching someone shuffle a deck of cards fast and with great precision. I couldn't walk away empty-handed. I needed a piece of this history to take with me, because in my heart I knew that like the fishing industry that was slowly disappearing here, someday the clicking of the crochet hooks would also stop.

# Regina in Porchetta

## Carp with Rosemary and Fennel

Serves 3 or 4

*2½ pounds
whole cleaned carp,
farm-raised trout,
or sea bass*

*4 ounces cooked ham
(optional)*

*2 sprigs fresh rosemary,
needles only*

*1 tablespoon
fresh fennel seeds*

*4 cloves garlic, peeled*

*Juice of 1 lemon*

*¼ cup extra-virgin
olive oil*

*Fine sea salt to taste*

*Lemon wedges*

Regina in porchetta *is a lovely classical Umbrian dish made with carp, which is revered by the fishermen of Isola Maggiore. If carp is not available, use whole farm-raised trout or sea bass. The delicacy of the fish is balanced by the savory stuffing of rosemary and fennel seeds, reminiscent of the preparation used for stuffing pork, hence the recipe's name. This dish is so easy to prepare for company that it will become a favorite.*

Preheat the oven to 400° F.

Lightly oil a baking dish large enough to hold the fish.

Wash and dry the fish in and out, and set aside.

Mince the ham, rosemary, fennel seeds, and garlic together in a food processor until a paste is formed. Stuff the paste into the cavity of the fish and place the fish in the prepared baking dish.

In a small bowl whisk together the lemon juice and olive oil until an emulsion is formed. Add the salt.

Bake the fish for 30 minutes, basting occasionally with the lemon and olive oil mixture. Carefully transfer the fish to a cutting board. Remove the head and discard. Scrape the skin away from the fish and discard. Carefully remove the filling from the cavity and place on a serving platter. Remove the fish meat with a couple of soup spoons and serve immediately along with some of the filling. Pass lemon wedges on the side for squeezing on top of the fish.

# *Tegamaccio*

## Lago Trasimeno Fish Stew

Serves 4 to 6

*This delicate fish stew is typical of what you will find on Isola Maggiore and Lago Trasimeno. The secret is to make sure the fish are all cut the same size and require the same amount of cooking time. Traditionally, a combination of eels, tench, perch, trout, whiting, and grayling is used, but you can use what is available. Just make sure to choose sturdy fish that will not break apart as it is cooked. Cusk and haddock as well as monkfish are also good for this recipe.*

Heat the olive oil in a saucepan. When it shimmers, add the parsley, red pepper flakes, and celery, and cook until the celery begins to soften. Stir in the garlic and cook until it softens. Stir in the tomatoes, wine, salt, and pepper. Lower the heat to a simmer and add the fish. Cook slowly, covered, for 5 to 8 minutes, or just until the fish flakes easily with a fork. Place a slice of bread in individual soup bowls and ladle the fish stew over the top. Pass olive oil to drizzle on top.

*¼ cup extra-virgin olive oil plus more for drizzling*

*⅓ cup minced parsley*

*½ teaspoon red pepper flakes*

*1 cup diced celery*

*2 cloves garlic, minced*

*6 cups pureed fresh plum tomatoes*

*½ cup dry white wine*

*Salt to taste*

*Freshly ground black pepper to taste*

*2 pounds assorted cleaned fish (monkfish, haddock, cusk), cut into 1-inch chunks*

*4 to 6 bread slices, toasted*

# Trota alla Griglia

## Grilled Trout

Serves 4

4 whole gutted trout

⅔ cup fresh
bread crumbs

Grated zest and juice of
1 large lemon

3 tablespoons
fresh minced parsley

¼ teaspoon fine sea salt

Freshly ground coarse
black pepper to taste

4 tablespoons
extra-virgin olive oil

4 sprigs fresh rosemary

*Fish from the Nera River are much appreciated for their juiciness, and like most Umbrian dishes, this grilled trout is seasoned very simply with parsley and rosemary. The key to this dish is to have a very hot grill ready and waiting.*

Rinse and dry the trout and set aside.

Mix the bread crumbs, zest, lemon juice, parsley, salt, pepper, and 2 tablespoons of the olive oil in a bowl. Stuff one-fourth of the mixture in the cavity of each trout.

Prepare a charcoal or gas grill. If you have a 4-place fish griller, lightly spray it with olive oil. Place the fish carefully in each of the 4 depressions and close the top. Place the fish griller on top of the grill. Dip the rosemary sprigs in the remaining olive oil and use to brush the fish as it cooks. Turn the griller to cook the other side. When the fish flakes easily with a fork, it is done. Remove the fish griller from the grill top, carefully open the griller, and remove the fish to a platter. Serve immediately.

To cook without a fish griller, place the fish directly on the grill top and use 2 wide-face metal spatulas to turn the fish as it cooks. Baste with the rosemary brush as above.

# When Saints Compete

*Crescia* (Cheese Bread)

*Fricco di Pollo all'Eugubina* (Gubbian-Style Stewed Chicken)

*Frittelle di Baccalà* (Fried Codfish Umbrian Style)

*T*hey are ardently competitive and revered like rock stars. They have fans in the millions. Their names are household words. Some say that they have touched their lives in miraculous ways, while others implore them daily to do the impossible. They are saints—Ubaldo, Antonio, and Georgio—and they are the honored holy ones in the ancient stone city of Gubbio.

*Gubbio's* Festa dei Ceri . . .
*a colorful step back in time*

Every May 15 they mesmerize the citizens of Gubbio and the world in a special way. In fact, no one from Gubbio would think of being anywhere else on that day but smack in the center of the Piazza Grande—young and old, packed like sardines, waiting in heightened anticipation to catch a glimpse of the saints as their likenesses are carried out of the austere-looking civic palace, the Palazzo dei Consoli, each one perched precariously on top of twenty-foot intricately carved, missile-shaped wooden candles called *ceri* that weigh about a thousand pounds each. Each saint is carried by teams of runners through narrow, eye-of-the-needle twisted streets up Mount Ingino, and is finally brought to rest at the summit in the Church of Saint Ubaldo.

It is a privilege for me to be in the midst of this reverent frenzy, to see up close what *La Corsa dei Ceri*—"the race of the candles"—means to the people of Gubbio. The plans for the festivities take all year. This is one of the oldest celebrations in Italy, even attracting people of Umbrian heritage from the United States and elsewhere. The event is documented in the *Tavole Eugubine,* the Eugubine Tablets, a set of prayers and rituals written in the Etruscan and Latin languages that dates from 250 to 150 B.C., housed in the Palazzo dei Consoli. Archaeologists have found evidence of the longevity of this event from sacrificial offerings made when it was a pagan celebration, before it was christianized in the year 1256.

May 15 is the eve of the anniversary of the death of Saint Ubaldo (1160), Gubbio's much-beloved bishop and patron saint. To prepare for the race, citizens from every walk of life take to the kitchens of the town's restaurants to cook a meatless feast for *la vigilia,* the vigil. In the kitchen of the Taverna del Lupo, a well-known restaurant, a group of men are singing as they prepare *baccala arrosta* (roasted codfish), wrap hunks of cheese bread, and prepare to sell the *baccala* to the public for a small sum. At the same time they prepare a feast for the privileged thousand or so guests, who along with town officials will eat together the next day in the Palazzo dei Consoli prior to the start of the race. The menu includes a cold salad of shrimp, calamari, and mussels; seafood risotto; boiled salmon with caper sauce; roast pork with rosemary; a frittata filled with seafood; mixed green salad; and a sponge cake filled with pastry cream in the shape of the *ceri* (a candle-shaped statue stand). Umbrian wines flow in abundance, and the crowd sings at a fever pitch—all in anticipation of five o'clock in the afternoon when the race of the saints begins. The irony of all this merrymaking is that the outcome of the race is already known, as it is each year. Saint Ubaldo is the declared winner even before the race begins. Of course this makes no sense to a foreigner, but it makes perfect sense to the people of Gubbio, who see this as an affirmation of their pride in being Eugubini.

Everyone participates in the event—from declaring allegiance to a favorite saint and wearing that saint's colors, to displaying the colors in flags that are draped from doorways, windows, and balconies. I buy a red-and-yellow scarf symbolizing Gubbio and Saint Ubaldo. Saint Anthony fans wear black, and Saint George, blue.

The crowd is at a fever pitch as the time grows closer for the race to begin and a downpour of red, yellow, black, and blue confetti rains down on the thousands of people squeezed into Piazza Grande. Drums begin to beat, trumpeters in red-and-white medieval costumes pump out their sounds, people begin to chant, and the bells of the campanile peal as the enormous doors of the civic palace open to announce each saint and its team of runners. I can feel the surge of energy in the crushing, deafening cry of the crowd as the first team races out carrying Saint Ubaldo high on top of his *cero*. He is whizzed through the crowd, resplendent in his pointed bishop's hat and clutching his gold staff, with his gold cape flapping in the breeze. He reminds me of a soft-souled Santa Claus with his snowy white beard and sweet face, but in fact he represents the absolute authority of the Church. Next comes Saint George, defender of the faith and symbol of the military, prancing on his mighty horse, his hands firmly on his silver shield and sword. He is all business, and the crowd rocks with enthusiasm. Then the gentle Saint Anthony, symbol of the working class, clothed in his humble brown garb, closes ranks and is paraded four times around the square, as is the tradition. Each saint is greeted with endless frenetic chants, and before the race begins, all the saints stop at various high windows and balconies along the narrow streets from which the citizens of Gubbio reach out to pin money to their clothes, touch them with reverence, give them a pat on the back, and encourage them to do their best.

At the stroke of five the race begins, with Saint Ubaldo leading the pack down the narrow, steep streets, followed by Saint George and Saint Anthony. They are cheered along the route to the church at the top of Mount Ingino as if no one knows who will win, but of course they do know; it is the way the race must be run, according to tradition. When darkness falls on Gubbio and the saints are once again returned to their resting places, the singing, dancing, and fun of this day continue long into the night. Soon plans will be made for next year's race, and the anticipation of who will win *La Corsa dei Ceri* will build once again in the souls and hearts of the Eugubini.

# *Crescia*

## Cheese Bread

Makes 1 large and 1 small bread

Crescia *is the cheese bread made in Umbria, and particularly in Gubbio, for* La Corsa dei Ceri, *the candle race in honor of Gubbio's patron, Saint Ubaldo. The domed loaf with its sunny yellow crumb rises high above its rim, and this is where it gets the name* crescia, *meaning to grow or rise. Flavored with flecks of coarse black pepper and several kinds of cheese including grated pecorino, chunks of mozzarella, and provolone, this impressive bread is best eaten warm.*

Spray a 6½ × 6½-inch high-sided pan and a 4 × 6½-inch high-sided pan with olive oil and set aside. The insert to a Crockpot works well for the larger loaf and brown paper lunch bags or panettone papers (special papers for baking panettone—see Mail Order Sources, page 199), work well for the smaller loaf.

Pour the water into a large bowl or into the bowl of a stand mixer. Stir in the yeast and allow to sit for 5 minutes. It will get chalky-looking, and bubbles should appear on the surface.

Beat the eggs with a whisk in a separate bowl. Whisk in the olive oil, black pepper, salt, and the grated cheese. Add to the yeast mixture and blend well. Begin adding the flour, 1 cup at a time, until a dough forms that does not stick to your hands. Use the paddle attachment if using a stand mixer to make the dough; the dough should wind itself around the paddle attachment when enough flour has been added. If doing this by hand, the job will be a little harder since this is a fairly heavy dough. Add just enough flour to

*1¾ cups warm water (110° F)*

*1 tablespoon active dry yeast*

*7 large eggs at room temperature*

*½ cup extra-virgin olive oil*

*1 teaspoon coarse black pepper*

*1 tablespoon salt*

*1 cup grated pecorino cheese*

*7 to 8 cups unbleached all-purpose flour*

*8 ounces mozzarella cheese, diced (1½ cups)*

*5 ounces provolone cheese, diced (1 cup)*

allow the dough to come away from the sides of the bowl. Transfer the dough to a lightly floured surface. Knead it a few times with your hands, then stretch the dough out and sprinkle the diced cheeses over the top. Fold the dough over the cheeses and knead them into the dough.

Coat a large bowl with olive oil and transfer the dough to the bowl. Cover tightly with plastic wrap and allow the dough to rise until doubled in size. This should take about 2 hours.

Punch down the dough with your hands and transfer it once again to a lightly floured surface. Knead for a few minutes. Cut two-thirds of the dough, knead it into a ball, and place it in the large pan. Knead the remaining one-third of the dough into a ball and place it in the smaller pan. Cover the pans with clean towels and allow the dough to rise for 30 to 35 minutes, or until they have risen two-thirds of the way up the sides of the pan.

Preheat the oven to 375° F.

Remove the top rack of the oven and set aside. Place the pans on a rack in the lowest position of the oven and bake the breads for 35 to 40 minutes, or until a skewer inserted in the center of the loaves comes out clean. The breads will rise to impressive heights, and if the tops brown too much before the breads are done, cover them loosely with a piece of aluminum foil.

Transfer the breads to a cooling rack and allow to cool until warm. Run a butter knife inside the pan to loosen the bread from the sides, then invert the pan and remove the bread. If using paper bags or panettone papers, there is no need to remove the bread from the papers.

*Tip: If available, use water drained from boiling potatoes in the recipe since potato water has a large amount of starch, and yeast likes to feed on it.*

# Fricco di Pollo all'Eugubina

## Gubbian-Style Stewed Chicken

Serves 4

*A fricco is a stew of sorts, and this easy-to-prepare Gubbian-style chicken stew highlights two classic Umbrian flavors: Orvieto Classico wine and rosemary. You'll see why both are so beloved and celebrated. This dish is even better if made the day before serving.*

Heat the olive oil in a large sauté pan and cook the onion over medium-low heat until soft and translucent. Raise the heat to medium-high and add the chicken pieces. Be sure they are well dried before adding them to the pan. Keep a bunch of paper towels handy for this. Cook, turning the pieces, until they are browned on all sides. This should take about 5 minutes.

Add the wine vinegar and allow it to evaporate. Lower the heat and add the sage and rosemary. Continue cooking over low heat for 15 minutes. Raise the temperature to high, add the wine, and allow it to evaporate. Pour in the pureed tomatoes. Season with salt and pepper, and continue cooking, uncovered, for 25 minutes, or until the sauce thickens and the chicken is tender when pierced with a fork.

Arrange the chicken on a platter and pour the sauce over the top. Serve immediately.

*¼ cup extra-virgin olive oil*

*1 large white onion, peeled and coarsely chopped*

*3½ pounds chicken, cut into pieces*

*¼ cup white wine vinegar*

*4 fresh sage leaves, crumbled*

*2 sprigs fresh rosemary*

*1 cup dry white wine, such as Orvieto Classico*

*4 large plum tomatoes, pureed and sieved to remove skin and seeds*

*Fine sea salt to taste*

*Freshly ground coarse black pepper to taste*

# Frittelle di Baccalà

## Fried Codfish Umbrian Style

Serves 4

*2 pounds air-dried codfish*

*1 large egg*

*1 cup milk or water*

*3 tablespoons flour*

*¼ teaspoon baking soda*

*¼ teaspoon salt*

*6 cups vegetable oil*

*Lemon wedges*

*Even though Umbria is landlocked, Lago Trasimeno near Perugia provides an excellent selection of freshwater fish with which the Umbrians create simple yet tasty dishes. Saltwater fish such as stockfish is also a favorite. This is air-dried cod (not to be confused with salted cod) that is presoaked to plump it up, then coated in a thin batter and fried. Enjoy it piping hot with a good squirt of fresh lemon juice and a dash of salt. Heaven!*

Place the fish in a casserole dish large enough to hold it in 1 layer. Cover the fish with water and let it soak overnight but change the water every few hours. The fish will rehydrate and plump up. The next day, rinse and dry the fish and cut it into 2-inch pieces. Set aside.

Make the batter by whisking together the egg and milk in a bowl until frothy.

Mix the flour, baking soda, and salt together in a small bowl. Whisk this into the milk mixture until a smooth, thin pancake-like batter is formed. A whisk will help prevent a lumpy batter. Cover and refrigerate the mixture for several hours or overnight. The batter will thicken.

When ready to fry the fish, heat the vegetable oil in a deep fryer to 375° F or use a wide, heavy-clad pan and a thermometer. Dip the fish pieces into the batter, a few at a time, shaking off the excess. Fry the fish until golden brown. Remove the fish with a slotted spoon or lift the wire basket from the deep fryer and put the fish on absorbent paper to drain. Keep the fish warm while the remaining pieces are cooked. Arrange the fish on a serving dish, sprinkle a little salt over the top, and serve immediately accompanied by lemon wedges.

*Tip: Keep the oven heated to 200° F, and as you cook the pieces, transfer them to a paper-lined baking sheet kept warm in the oven until all the pieces have been fried.*

# A Wine Story

*Scaloppine di Vitello ai Capperi* (Veal Cutlet in Caper Sauce)

*Involtini di Carne con Prosciutto* (Meat Rolls Stuffed with Ham and Herbs)

*Pere al Sagrantino* (Pears Poached in Sagrantino Wine)

*Zuppa di Risina Il Bacco Felice* (Bacco Felice–Style Barley Soup)

*Zuppa di Risina e Gamberetti* (Shrimp Soup with Orzo and Farro)

*I* would trust anyone who had the last name of *di Dio* (of God) to tell me about Umbrian wines, so when I met Maurizio di Dio, the manager of the Arnaldo Caprai winery in the lofty wine zone of Montefalco, I knew that I was in good hands to learn about the most famous vines cultivated here to make wine called Sagran-

*Cent'anni . . . may you live a hundred years.*

tino. Maurizio is an enthusiastic young man full of knowledge about wine. He tells me that Sagrantino is a wine derived from a native vine that was brought to this area by Franciscan friars returning from Asia Minor. It is said it was originally a sacramental wine used at Mass, hence its name. At one time Sagrantino was produced exclusively using the *passito* method, which meant drying the grapes on wooden trellises to concentrate and preserve their natural sugar, which in turn produced a sweet wine. Today the *passito* method is no longer in vogue, and Sagrantino is a dry (*secco*) red, tannic, DOCG wine. (DOCG stands for *Denominazione di Origine Controllata Garantita,* which means a governing body oversees and sets the standards under which this wine is produced.) Other wines produced include Montefalco Rosso DOCG, made from Sangiovese grapes and a percentage of Sagrantino grapes, and Montefalco Bianco, a wine made from the Grechetto and Trebbiano grapes. It is a beautiful straw color, and has fruity flavors of apples and apricots.

Maurizio and I tasted each of these wines, and all the while thoughts swirled in my mind as to what dishes I could make to complement them. I admit that I am partial to reds, and when I mentioned this to Maurizio, he looked me straight in the eye and said, "All wine in Italy is red." I felt as if I had truly honored my Italian heritage!

After the tasting and a tour of the winery, Maurizio suggested lunch in nearby Foligno at an *enoteca*, or wine bar. When we entered the quaint and boisterous *enoteca*—called Il Bacco Felice, meaning the happy Bacchus, who is, of course, the god of wine—I knew we were in for a good time. We were greeted by the equally charming and boisterous Salvatore Denaro, a Sicilian by birth with a jovial laugh and a ton of generosity and hospitality. The *enoteca*'s walls were literally covered in graffiti, and wine bottles lined them from one end to the other like a shield of soldiers. There was room to seat only about fifteen people, and the place was very popular with locals.

Salvatore no sooner had greeted us than the food began to arrive at our table. Delicious *panzanella* (bread salad) came first, made with crumbled dense bread, a variety of raw vegetables, and the most incredible-tasting *pomodorini* (small tomatoes), all combined with a spicy Umbrian olive oil. Plates of *prosciutto crudo* made the rounds, then steaming bowls of lentil soup and another soup, made with an orzo type of pasta called risina, tiny shrimp, and farro. All were exquisite, all reflected the use of local Umbrian products, and all were accompanied by the wines of the Arnaldo Caprai estate. I was as happy as Bacchus.

# *Scaloppine di Vitello ai Capperi*

## Veal Cutlet in Caper Sauce

Serves 4

*The Umbrian dry white wine Montefalco Bianco is used to make this quick veal scaloppine dish. You can also substitute chicken or boneless pork; just make sure you are buying thinly sliced and pounded slices of meat no more than one-fourth inch thick. Buy good capers in salt and rinse them well before using. These little power-packed buds grow in craggy rocks in the Mediterranean and are used to flavor many Italian dishes.*

*1 pound (8 slices) thinly sliced veal, chicken, or pork*

*⅓ cup flour*

*½ cup extra-virgin olive oil*

*⅔ cup Montefalco Bianco or other dry white wine*

*Juice of 1 large lemon*

*1 tablespoon finely minced capers*

*2 tablespoons finely minced parsley*

*Fine sea salt to taste*

*Freshly ground black pepper to taste*

Dry the meat slices well with paper towels. Place in a plastic bag with the flour and shake the bag to coat the slices evenly. Shake off the excess flour and set the meat aside.

Heat the olive oil in a sauté pan, and when it begins to shimmer, brown the meat slices in batches. Do this quickly, and do not over-cook them or they will toughen. As you cook them, transfer them to a heatproof dish and keep them warm in the oven.

Pour the wine and lemon juice into the pan and cook, scraping up the browned bits in the pan. Stir in the capers and parsley, and cook 1 minute more. Season with salt and pepper. Pour the sauce over the veal and serve immediately.

# *Involtini di Carne con Prosciutto*

## Meat Rolls Stuffed with Ham and Herbs

Serves 4

*8 thin veal, pork, or chicken slices cut for scaloppine*

*8 thin slices of prosciutto*

*2 tablespoons finely crushed juniper berries*

*8 whole sage leaves*

*Freshly ground black pepper to taste*

*Fine sea salt to taste*

*Extra-virgin olive oil*

*½ cup Montefalco Rosso or other red wine*

Involtini *are stuffed, rolled bundles with a savory filling. These have a nice woodsy flavor provided by fresh sage and juniper berries. Montefalco Rosso is used to make the sauce, but any good dry red wine will suffice. This is a great dish for company.*

Lay the meat pieces flat. Top each one with a slice of prosciutto, a little of the crushed juniper berries, a sage leaf, a grinding of pepper, and a sprinkling of salt. Roll up each piece to form a little bundle. This is the *involtino*. Tie the *involtini* with kitchen string and place in a baking dish.

Preheat the oven to 350° F.

Brush the *involtini* with olive oil and bake for 5 minutes. Pour in the wine and continue baking 7 minutes more. Baste the bundles occasionally with the wine and bake about 12 minutes more. Serve hot.

*Note: Juniper berries are in the spice section of most grocery stores. Use a mortar and pestle to crush them or use a small spice grinder.*

# Pere al Sagrantino

## Pears Poached in Sagrantino Wine

Serves 4

*W*hen I mentioned to Maurizio di Dio that I like to poach pears in *Sagrantino, he winced and said, no, solo da bere—only to drink. I think I need to make him these poached pears in Sagrantino and turn him into a believer. If Sagrantino is not available, use a Barbera wine.*

*4 slightly ripe Anjou, Williams, or Bartlett pears, peeled and with stem top*

*4 cups Sagrantino wine*

*¾ cup sugar*

*One 3-inch piece of cinnamon stick*

*Zest of 1 large lemon*

Place the pears in a saucepan just large enough to accommodate them upright. Mix the wine and sugar together and add it with the rest of the ingredients. Cover the pan and simmer the pears until a small knife is inserted easily into the pears. Remove them with a slotted spoon to a dish and let them cool.

While the pears cool, boil the wine until it is reduced by half. Set aside.

Cut the pears in half lengthwise. Use a small spoon to remove the inner core and seeds. Place 2 halves on each of 4 individual serving dishes, or leave the pears whole.

Pour a little of the wine sauce over the top of each dish and serve.

*V*ariation: *For an elegant presentation, wet the rims of sorbet or ice cream bowls and dip the rims in coarse white sugar. Add a whole pear and some of the wine sauce to each bowl.*

# Zuppa di Risina Il Bacco Felice

## Bacco Felice–Style Barley Soup

Makes about 1½ quarts

*5 cups chicken broth, homemade or canned, low sodium*

*¾ cup pearl barley or orzo*

*1 tablespoon extra-virgin olive oil*

*1 large carrot, scraped and diced*

*2 medium ribs celery, diced*

*1 medium onion, peeled and diced*

*4 ounces chunk prosciutto, diced*

*1 teaspoon dried hot red pepper flakes*

*20 small cherry tomatoes, cut in half*

*⅛ teaspoon dried oregano*

*¾ teaspoon celery salt*

*Salt to taste*

*S*alvatore Denaro makes this delicious and quick-to-prepare soup with risina, a grain that looks a lot like barley or orzo. Since risina is not easy to come by, I use pearl barley, and the results are just as good. I had this soup, sometimes referred to as la risina del Trasimeno, in Salvatore's eclectic enoteca in the sleepy town of Foligno. As in many Umbrian recipes, the ubiquitous prosciutto shows up, adding flavor and texture.

Pour the chicken broth into a 2-quart saucepan and bring to a boil. Stir in the barley and cook about 20 minutes, or just until *al dente*.

While the barley is cooking, heat the olive oil in a sauté pan and stir in the carrot, celery, and onion. Cook, stirring occasionally, until the vegetables start to soften. Stir in the prosciutto and hot red pepper flakes and continue cooking for a couple of minutes. Stir in the tomatoes, oregano, celery salt, and salt.

Stir the vegetable mixture into the barley, cover the saucepan, lower the heat, and simmer for 3 or 4 minutes. Serve immediately.

# Zuppa di Risina e Gamberetti

## Shrimp Soup with Orzo and Farro

Makes 1¾ quarts

*This soup is another of Salvatore Denaro's signature dishes in the* enoteca. *I find the tiny shrimp* (gamberetti) *swimming in a tomato-based broth different, delicious, and filling. Though this soup takes more time to prepare than* zuppa di risina Il Bacco Felice *(page 186), it can be considered a meal in itself. I have adapted the recipe by using orzo in place of the risina. Tiny dried white beans can also be substituted. Farro packs this soup with both flavor and nutrition. Soak the farro the day before and cook the orzo or beans ahead to cut down on the cooking time.*

Pour the orzo into a saucepan and cover with 3 cups of cold water. Bring to a boil and cook about 15 to 20 minutes, just until *al dente,* firm but cooked. (If you are using beans, soak them overnight, then cook them about 30 minutes, or until tender but not mushy.) Drain and set aside.

Soak the farro overnight, drain, and transfer it to the saucepan used to cook the orzo. Cover the farro with 3 cups of cold water and bring to a boil. Cook about 25 minutes, or just until the grains are cooked through but still remain firm. Drain and set aside.

Place the tomatoes in a food processor, food mill, or blender and puree until smooth. Pour the pulp into a fine-mesh strainer placed over a bowl. Press on the pulp with a spoon to release its juice. Discard the seeds and skins. There should be about 2 cups of tomato juice. If not, add water. Set aside.

*½ cup orzo or
    small dried white
    beans*

*½ cup farro*

*2½ pounds
    plum tomatoes,
    coarsely chopped*

*2 tablespoons
    extra-virgin olive oil
    plus more for drizzling*

*2 stalks celery,
    thinly sliced*

*1 small onion, minced*

*¼ cup minced parsley*

*4 cups hot chicken broth*

*2 teaspoons celery salt*

*½ teaspoon sea salt*

*Freshly ground
    black pepper to taste*

*1 pound small cooked
    shrimp (see Note)*

Heat the olive oil in a 2-quart saucepan and stir in the celery, onion, and parsley. Cook until the vegetables soften. Pour in the chicken broth, reserved tomato juice, celery salt, salt, and pepper, and bring to a boil. Lower the heat and cook the mixture, covered, for 5 minutes. Stir in the orzo and farro. Stir in the shrimp. Cook over low heat for 3 or 4 minutes; do not let the soup boil, or the shrimp will become tough.

Ladle the soup into bowls and pass olive oil to drizzle on top.

*Variation: Add small broccoli florets to the soup.*

*Note: If you cannot find small shrimp, buy the 20-40 count and cut them in half lengthwise.*

# The Umbrian Pantry

The world of food has gotten very small. It's easier than ever to get ingredients to create all sorts of international dishes at home. Umbrian cooking is so basic that the only things you will not be able to find are some of the cured meats, which because of FDA regulations are not allowed into this country, and succulent *porchetta* (pork). But with the substitutions given in the recipes, you will be able to prepare much of what makes up home-style Umbrian cooking. Here are some of the basic ingredients, many of which can be kept on hand.

## *Dry and Jarred Staples*

Umbrian olive oil
Lentils
Dried beans including fava, chickpeas, and small white beans
Farro and farro flour
Wheat berries
Truffle paste
Dried pastas including strangozzi, umbricelli, orzo, and spaghetti
Almonds, walnuts, and pine nuts
Perugina baking chocolate and cocoa
Dried yeast
Candied orange and lemon peels
Citron
Anchovies in oil
Red wine vinegar
Capers in salt

Marjoram
Garlic
Fennel seeds
Raisins
Honey
Dried porcini mushrooms
Fine and coarse sea salt
Unbleached all-purpose flour

## Cheeses

*Formaggio al tartufo nero*
Mozzarella
Parmigiano-Reggiano
Pecorino
Ricotta
Ricotta Salata
Scamorza
Gorgonzola
Feta
Provolone

## Cured Meats

Capicolla
*Salame locale*
*Prosciutto crudo*

## Vegetables

Garlic
Onions
Celery
Carrots
Cherry tomatoes

Plum tomatoes
Fennel
Red potatoes
Bitter lettuces
   Arugula
   Spinach
   Chicory
Beets
Broccoletti

## *Wines*

Rosso di Montefalco
Sagrantino di Montefalco
Orvieto Classico
Orvieto Rosso
Torgiano Rosso Riserva

# Umbrian Restaurants

For those of you lucky enough to be planning a trip to Umbria, here are some of my favorite places to eat in the region. For the rest of us, consider this list a bit of "armchair eating."

## Assisi

**La Stalla**, Via Eremo delle Carceri. Phone 075-813636*
A rustic eatery with communal outdoor tables. Grilled foods include chicken, pork, and pheasant.

## Campello sul Clitunno

**Pettino**, Frazione Pettino 31. Phone 0743-276021
Delicious truffle dishes can be found in this quiet spot. Local cured meats are a specialty.

## Foligno

**Il Bacco Felice**, Via Garibaldi 75. Phone 0742-341019
This wonderful wine *enoteca* has a wide price range. It has a great selection of cheeses and bean and farro soups.

*Note: These are phone numbers to use when dialing in Italy. If calling from the United States, add international code 011, followed by Italy's country code 39, and delete the first zero listed, which is part of the local code.

## Gubbio

**Taverna del Lupo**, Via Giovanni Ansidel 21. Phone 0759-274368
Features traditional Umbrian dishes, *imbrecciata* (a hearty bean
soup), guinea hen, *coniglio in porchetta* (stuffed rabbit), and specialty pastas such as *umbricelli*. A fabulous restaurant with great
intimate decor.
**Bossone Garden**, Via XX Settembre 22. Phone 0759-221246
A beautiful setting. Has typical Umbrian dishes, grilled meats, local
pasta, and black truffles.

## Lizori

**Ristorante Camesena**, Pissignano Alto. Phone 0743-520340
This beautifully appointed restaurant sits high on a hilltop over-
looking Pissignano Alto. Dishes with farro, homemade pasta, lentils, and hearth-baked breads are a specialty.

## Montefalco

**Federico 11**, Piazza del Comune-Vicolo Valenti. Phone 0742-
378902
Umbrian soups, pasta dishes, and great wine selections.

## Norica

**Dal Francese**, Via Riguardati 16. Phone 0743-816290
Here pork dishes are king, plus there is local salame, proscuitto,
lentil soup, pork on the grill, and black truffles.

## Orvieto

**I Sette Consoll**, Piazza Sant'Angelo. Phone 0763-343911
A Michelin star restaurant with rabbit dishes, ravoili with chicken
liver mousse, and lamb chops stuffed with foie gras.

**Osteria Dell'Angelo**, Piazza XXIX Marzo. Phone 0763-341805
Pasta dishes and soups are outstanding; also duck breast in truffle sauce, lentils, and rabbit.

### Perugia

**La Taverna**, Via delle Streghe. Phone 0755-724128
This elegant restaurant serves typical dishes including grilled local pecorino cheese, grilled meats, filled pasta dishes, and Colfiorito lamb.

**Antica Trattoria**, San Lorenzo Piazza Danti. Phone 075-5721956
Traditional Umbrian dishes include lentils, stuffed pastas, and duck.

**Trattoria Dell' Orso**, Via della Misericordia. Phone 0763-341642
You'll find farro soup with vegetables and fennel seed, roast pork dishes, and pasta ortolana featuring vegetables in season.

### Spoleto

**Ristorante Apollinare**, Via Santa Agata. Phone 0743-223256
Grain-based dishes, *strangozzi,* hearty soups, and black truffle–laced dishes are featured in a country setting.

### Torgiano

**Tre Vaselle**, Via Garibaldi. Phone 0759-880447
Local fare here includes black truffles, *strangozzi, porchetta,* and locally cured meats.

### Trevi

**Vecchia Posta**, Piazza Mazzini 14. Phone 0742-381690
This family-run restaurant serves seasonal fare and classic Umbrian dishes including omelettes made with truffles, cured meats, homemade pasta, and Trevi's famed black celery.

# Umbria Web Sites

Here is a list of useful Web sites pertaining to Umbria, covering its foods, wine, art, and places to stay. I have also included Web sites of Italian specialty stores in the States that carry Umbrian products or provide travel to Umbria.

**www.CaravellaItalia.com**
Small group travel company based in Philadelphia with special ties to Umbria.

**www.chefwalter.com**
Walter Potenza takes groups to Gubbio and teaches Umbrian cooking.
Phone 401-273-2652

**www.dairyfreshcandies.com**
Boston store specializing in Italian imported products including dried beans and Umbrian olive oils.

**www.growitalian.com**
A wonderful source for garden seeds from Italy. Reasonable prices and great variety. Seeds from Italy, P.O. Box 149, Winchester, Massachusetts 01890.

**www.hostetler.net/cgi-shl/dbml.exe?template-hostetler/italy/dbm**
A database of Umbrian festivals, including the *Corsa dei Ceri*, organized by region and month, plus links to official Web sites and contact information.

**www.ilbuongustaio.com**

Information on foods and related products.

**www.made-in-italy.com**

General information site for over sixteen regions in Italy. A good site with many tips.

**www.mencarelligroup.com**

Information on travel and accommodations in Gubbio and other areas of Umbria, plus data on cooking classes in Umbria.

**www.newadvent.org/cathen**

Biographies of Saint Francis, Saint Clare, and Saint Ubaldo.

**www.seeumbria.com**

Umbrian olive oils from a company based in Florida. Contact Luca Contessa, G. L. Products and Services, Inc., Boca Raton, Florida 33433.

**www.umbria.org**

Source for hotels and vacation rental properties.

**www.umbriadoc.com/Eng**

Information on Umbrian wines, truffles, lentils, and cheeses.

**www.urbani.com**

Source for Umbrian food products including black truffles and olive oil.

Phone 800-281-2330

# Mail Order Sources

Here are some excellent sources for ingredients, cookware, and other products useful for anyone preparing the recipes in this book.

**Balducci's**
424 Avenue of the Americas
New York, New York 10011
800-225-3822 or 1-800-BALDUCCI/Catalog
**www.balducci.com**
A treasure trove of Italian products, including farro, orzo, and chickpeas.

**Ciao Times**
P.O. Box 891
Durham, New Hampshire 03824
**www.ciaoitalia.com**
Mail order and Web site order for *Ciao Italia* products that include embroidered and personalized aprons, *Ciao Italia* watches, and mugs.

**Claudio's King of Cheese**
929 South Ninth Street
South Philadelphia, Pennsylvania 19147
Has a wide variety of Italian cheeses, prosciutto, salame, capicolla, and olives.

**Clay Angel**
Sante Fe, New Mexico
505-471-4899

**Email:clayangel@mindspring.com**
Source for Deruta pottery from Franco Mari shop in Deruta, Italy.

**Colavita Pasta**
2537 Brunswick Avenue
Linden, New Jersey 07036
**www.colavita.com**
All cuts of dried pasta plus olives, tomatoes, vinegars, and olive oil.

**Coluccio and Sons**
1214 60th Street
Brooklyn, New York 11219
718-436-6700
A wide variety of Italian products, including cheeses and cured meats. A great source for dried beans, wheat berries, farro, farro flour, and frozen fava beans.

**Dean & Deluca**
Catalog Orders
P.O. Box 20810
Wichita, Kansas 67208-6810
**www.deandeluca.com**
Italian-cured meats, cheeses, and cookware.

**DiBruno Brothers**
109 South 18th Street
Philadelphia, Pennsylvania 19103
215-665-9220/Catalog
Cured meats, pancetta, cheeses, and olive oils, pasta, anchovies, capers.

**Fante's**
1006 South 9th Street
Philadelphia, Pennsylvania 19147
800-878-5557

**fantes.com**

Large selection of baking needs, pasta machines and motor attachments, and cookware.

**Gallucci's Italian Foods**

6610 Euclid Avenue

Cleveland, Ohio 44103

216-881-0045/Catalog

An all-encompassing Italian grocery store featuring everything from pizzelle irons to cheeses from all over Italy, and olive oils, preserved fruits, dried beans, chickpeas, and lentils.

**Gasparro's**

Atwells Avenue

Providence, Rhode Island

401-421-4170

Wines, spirits, and Alchermes.

**Joe Pace and Sons**

42 Cross Street

Boston, Massachusetts 02113

617-227-9673 or 781-231-9599

Cured meats, cheeses, pancetta, lentils, dried beans, Italian flours, truffle paste, pasta, nuts, candied peels, and spices.

**King Arthur Flour**

P.O. Box 1010

Norwich, Vermont 05055

802-649-3881 or 800-827-6836 (Baker's Catalog)

**www.kingarthurflour.com**

All types of Italian flours, unbleached all-purpose flour, extracts, baking supplies, candied fruits, sea salts, turbinado sugar, dried yeast, wheat gluten, and baking chocolate.

**Kitchen Etc.**
32 Industrial Drive
Exeter, New Hampshire 03833
800-232-4070/Catalog
**www.kitchenetc.com**
A full line of baking and cookware, small appliances, pasta machines, kitchen tools, knives, and gadgets.

**Seeds from Italy**
P.O. Box 149
Winchester, Massachusetts 01890/Catalog
**www.growitalian.com**
A wonderful source for garden seeds from Italy. Reasonable prices and great variety.

**The Spice Corner**
904 South Ninth Street
Philadelphia, Pennsylvania
800-SPICES or 215-925-1661
**www.thespicecorner.com**

**Urbani Truffle Company**
29-24 40th Avenue
Long Island, New York 11101
800-281-2330
www.urbani.com
Fresh truffles, truffle paste.

**Venda Ravioli Company**
265 Atwells Avenue
Providence, Rhode Island 02903
401-421-9105
www.vendaravioli.com
Full line of imported Italian food products, including Umbrian olive oil, Deruta ceramic ware, cheeses, pastas, truffle paste, olives, capers, vinegars, and biscotti.

**Zabar's**
2245 Broadway
New York, New York 10024
212-787-2000 or 800-697-6301/Catalog
**www.zabars.com**
A wide variety of imported Italian cheeses, olives, and olive oils.

# English Index

# Italian Index